BRIDGING THE FINANCIAL GAP

FOR DENTISTS

What Every Dentist
Should Know About
Managing Money

Larry Mathis, CFP®

BRIDGING THE FINANCIAL GAP
FOR DENTISTS
What Every Dentist Should Know About Managing Money
Larry Mathis, CFP®

ISBN: 1-933596-82-1 Paperback
ISBN: 1-933596-81-3 Hardcover
ISBN: 1-933596-83-X eBook
ISBN: 1-933596-84-8 Audio

Morgan James books may be purchased for educational, business, or sales promotional use. For information please write: Special Markets Department, Morgan James Publishing LLC, 1225 Franklin Ave, Ste. 325, Garden City, NY 11530.

Published by:

MORGAN · JAMES
THE ENTREPRENEURIAL PUBLISHER™

Morgan James Publishing, LLC
1225 Franklin Ave. Ste. 325
Garden City, NY 11530-1693
Toll Free 800-485-4943
www.MorganJamesPublishing.com

Interior Design by:
Norma Strange
Strange View
www.strangeview.com

Habitat
for Humanity®
Peninsula
Building Partner

*For the love of my life, Rhonda,
and to our three sons
Trent, Jared and Cameron.*

You are my reasons for all I do.

*Thank you for your patience
and your encouragement.
I love you all
"higher than the sky and deeper than the sea."*

Table of Contents

Acknowledgements

I would personally like to thank the following people for their help throughout my career in the financial services industry. Thanks to all of you for the positive impact you have had on both my professional and personal life:

Jim Rhode, CSP, Chairman Smart Practice
Naomi Rhode, RDH, CSP, CPAE, Speaker Hall of Fame
Ben Lontock
Dr. Randy Womack
Dennis Rogers, CPA, CFP®
Frank Kirby
Sam Post, LUTCF, CLTC
David Lavin, CLU, ChFC, CLTC

In addition I would like to thank the following people for their encouragement and their valuable input throughout the writing process. Your help made getting this book to print possible. Thanks to all of you!

Brett F. Sperbeck, DDS
Kirk J. Anderton, DDS, MS
Alan Wilson, Attorney at Law
Pepper Veatch – Pepper Practice Transitions
Norma Strange – Strange View Marketing & Advertising
Alan Gold, CPA – Matthews, Gold, Kennedy & Snow
Scott Pilchard, Vice President – Manning & Napier
Jeff Dickerson – Glendale Insurance
Robert Schlangen, United Planners Financial Services of America
Colleen A. Jacobs & Fani Daskalakis – Morningstar®

Special thanks to Bill Bachrach, CSP and David Bach, both of whom motivated me to write this book through their training, inspiration and example.

Foreword

Having spoken in the dental profession for more than 30 years, and creating SmartPractice, we know and love the dental profession! We know the strengths of our professional colleagues and we know where counsel and advice are needed and appreciated.

One of the real challenges for us all as persons and "professionals" is to recommend carefully. That is anything but tenuous in this case! This is an overwhelming and enthusiastic recommendation and invitation to the wealth of information and counsel that *Bridging the Financial Gap for Dentists* will provide you.

We have known and worked with Larry Mathis for many years. Larry's counsel goes beyond the knowledge of most investment advisors and CPA's because he cares intensely, and has rich wisdom in guiding people to making financial decisions based on what is important to them. The goal is financial independence, yes, but far beyond independence. The goal is to help people self discover "why they do what they do" and to know "what is really important for them in life."

Truly, it goes far beyond the process to the purpose! Much has been written about purpose in life—being purpose driven. But how often does a financial advisor care to slow down and ask us the really hard questions about what is important, why it is important, and then challenge us to make financial decisions that will help us reach those goals?

We would encourage you to not just pick up this book for a quick glance but to savor each word with determined application. Don't even think of putting this book on your library shelf until you have a purpose to *save,* a decision to *spend wisely*, and a plan that moves your life financially beyond success to significance.

Every word is wise—read, savor, apply and enjoy the journey!

— *Naomi Rhode, RDH, CSP, CPAE Speaker Hall of Fame*
Jim Rhode, CSP, Chairman SmartPractice

Introduction

What is the Purpose of This Book?

In the past 17 years I have met and worked with scores of dental professionals. I have assisted some who are just getting started in practice and others who have been practicing for 30 or more years. I have worked with dentists who are deeply in debt as well as those who have accumulated substantial wealth from their practices. I have consulted with general dentists and dental professionals in every area of dental specialty, from orthodontists, endodontists, and periodontists, to oral and maxillofacial surgeons, pediatric dentists, and yes, even prosthodontists!

For those of my clients who are reading this book, I want to tell you that I have thoroughly enjoyed working with you over the years. In doing so, I have developed some of the best friendships of my life and for this I am thankful to the entire dental profession.

Picture this scenario. You are standing in line somewhere, maybe at the grocery store or at the movies, and as you are standing there, you begin to talk with the person next to you. As a dentist what is one of the first things you notice about that person? It's their smile, right? And I am sure there are times when you see someone with a less than perfect smile, that you say to yourself, "If only they knew what I (or one of your colleagues) could do for them. If only they knew how I could change their lives!"

Sometimes I, too, think the same thing after talking with someone. "If only they knew how I could help them improve their life." The truth is sometimes I even think, "I wonder if they can really afford that car, or that house or boat. Do they have all that stuff paid for or are they leveraged to the hilt? Do they sleep well at night or do they go to bed at night worrying about money?" It's funny (maybe even a little weird) but I actually do think about these things.

This is one reason I decided to write this book.

I have no doubt in my mind that if someone really knew how much I could help them with their finances, there would be no stopping them from wanting my help. Well, I can't personally work with everyone, but in writing this book, I know I can at least give some positive direction to dental professionals in need of financial planning assistance.

The idea for this book came about in an interesting manner. I was in my office when I received a phone call from my good friend Jim Rhode, the founder of SmartPractice (now SmartHealth), who I met 15 years ago through an introduction from Dr. Randy Womack, a successful orthodontist in Phoenix. Jim called to ask me if I would be willing to speak to a group of young dentists that he was working with. I agreed and Jim immediately then asked, "What's the title of your presentation?" One thing I can say about Jim Rhode is that when he gets a commitment, he's not going to let you off the hook. I said to him, "I don't know, Jim. You just asked me two minutes ago if I would speak. Tell me a little about who I will be speaking to." Jim explained that it was a group of young dentists who were in the early years of their practice. He mentioned that several of them were working to get their school debt paid off and he really wanted to be sure they got started out on the right financial track.

So I told Jim that I would start by talking about how to get out of debt and proceed to how to get on the track to wealth accumulation. I made up a title. "How about, 'Debt Management to Wealth Management, Twelve Things Every Dental Professional Needs to Know About Their Personal Finances,'" I said. Jim thought that would be great and we worked out the details of the date and time.

About twenty minutes later, I was having lunch with an associate, Frank Kirby, and related the phone conversation I had with Jim to Frank. Frank said, "That sounds like a great opportunity." He then said, "Debt Management to Wealth Management? Basically what you want to do is bridge the gap between the two." "That's exactly it, Frank! That's exactly what I want to do, show them how to *Bridge the Financial Gap!*" There couldn't be a more perfect title for a talk on finances to a group of dentists.

I had been working on another book relating to personal finances for some time. But the more I thought about it, the more I thought, "What a fun thing to do. I'll write a book about what I do. I will write about the process I use when helping my clients make smart choices with their money. It will relate specifically to the dental profession and I will call it

Bridging the Financial Gap for Dentists!" I think it's a great title and I hope you as a reader find that the content lives up to the title. Thanks, Frank!

Let's be clear what this book is and what it is not.

Before we get started though, I think you should know a few things. First of all, this book is not a book about picking the best stocks for your investment portfolio. It's not about how to beat the system with convoluted tax schemes. It's also not intended to teach you everything you need to know about financial planning so you can "do it yourself." It is, however, designed to help you make smart financial decisions in several key areas that nearly every dental professional is faced with at some point in their careers.

Bridging the Financial Gap for Dentists is intended to achieve these three goals:

1. Help you avoid costly mistakes that may prevent you from achieving your personal and financial goals in the time frame you are hoping for.
2. Assist you in maximizing your wealth potential, by making smart choices with your money, regardless of where you stand financially at this moment.
3. Help you discover how to live your life based upon those things that you value most and inspire you to develop a financial strategy to help you enjoy them to the fullest.

For the most part, the discussions detailed in this book will address financial issues most people will face during their lifetimes, but they are tailored specifically to the dental profession. Ultimately, it is my hope that *Bridging the Financial Gap for Dentists* will

Simplify and improve the lives of dental professionals
by inspiring them to implement financial strategies
based upon those things that are most important to them in life.

You're In the Right Profession

I graduated from Arizona State University in 1984. While I was there, I was very fortunate to take several history courses from a very gifted professor by the name of Dr. Brad Luckingham. Dr. Luckingham, a very distinguished Bostonian, was one of, if not the best teacher I have ever experienced. He's the type of lecturer who got us into the lesson. His classes were always full and very popular. He would have us in the pubs of 18th Century New England planning the Revolutionary War. One day, while in his class, Dr. Luckingham was lecturing and right in the middle of the battle of Gettysburg, he stopped, looked out at the class and said, "Dentistry. Dentistry is where it's at! What are you doing sitting in American History class? You should be studying dentistry!" He then continued on with his lecture, without missing a beat.

The following semester, I was sitting in Dr. Luckingham's Arizona History class and this time he got us coming across the Arizona desert with General Crook and his soldiers. Right in the middle of his lecture, he stops. "Orthodontics! Orthodontics! Specialize!" He then proceeds with the rest of the history lesson.

It's obvious that Dr. Luckingham was having some sort of experience with the dental profession during that period, most likely with his children. But, just in case you're wondering if you are in the right profession, Dr. Luckingham believes you are! "Dentistry! Dentistry is where it's at!"

Design and Implement the Financial Treatment Plan
What does all of this have to do with *Bridging the Financial Gap for Dentists*? Through my work with dental professionals I have found that many of them wind up reacting to events (and to sales people) instead of proactively designing a financial plan and then implementing the plan. They can be very much like some patients I'm sure you have dealt with.

Tell me, has this ever happened to you? You have a new patient (we'll call her Mary) who comes in for an initial exam. You, of course, are prepared to complete a comprehensive exam, which includes an evaluation of Mary's teeth, and gum tissue as well as a full series of radiographs (x-rays). During the initial exam you notice Mary has a broken tooth, which is in need of immediate attention. Because Mary has a broken tooth, you are planning to prepare for a crown. As you finish explaining to Mary the protocol for a crown, her response to you is, "Can't you just fill the tooth?"

You then go through the process of explaining to Mary why it is important to have a crown vs. a filling. You explain to her that although the crown will be more expensive ($800), she will be much better off in the long run. Her response this time is, "I think I'll just have a filling for now; maybe we can do the crown later if the filling doesn't work." So, you do the filling for $180 and Mary leaves happy and relieved that she didn't need a crown.

You haven't seen her for two years when, one day, Mary returns to your office. She is experiencing pain and discomfort on that previously filled tooth. Of course, she's upset that she's back in your office again and though she may not verbalize it to you, she, of course, blames you. After all, if you had done the filling right, she wouldn't have had to come back. After your evaluation, you now explain to Mary that, in addition to needing a crown, she is also going to need to make an appointment with an endodontist for a root canal and then afterward you will be able to complete her crown for her. Her total bill now will be $1,900 ($1,100 for the root canal and $800 for the crown). However, this time when Mary leaves she's not so happy. In fact she's upset with you, because in her mind you should have done the job right in the first place!

The ideal patients for most dentists are those who come in and allow the dentist to design a comprehensive treatment plan and then implement the plan accordingly. In our example above, Mary would not be considered an ideal patient. However, the fact is most dental professionals act very much the same way with their finances as Mary does with her teeth. Too many dental professionals are on the lookout for the fastest and cheapest way to solve a financial issue, be it purchasing disability insurance or selecting their investment option to fund their retirement plan. The truth is, as dental professionals they would be much better off if they would simply design a financial plan and implement it in a systematic fashion. In short, they should act in the same fashion regarding their finances, as they want their patients to do with their dental health.

It is not my intention to condemn the dental profession for lack of financial savvy. Dental professionals tend to be no different than anyone else when it comes to dealing with their finances. I am focusing on dental professionals because I have worked in this field for many years and I understand the unique challenges of financial planning within the dental profession. Just like financial planning, dentistry is based on the premise of providing service that helps to improve the current lives of people, with the added goal of long-term health. And though our professions are very different in the actual services we provide to our patients/clients, I think you will find many similarities between our professions as you continue to read *Bridging the Financial Gap for Dentists.*

What is Financial Planning?

Before we go any further, I think it's important for me to define financial planning. Financial planning is a term that is misused in my industry. Unfortunately the majority of people who call themselves financial planners are not truly planners at all. They are financial sales people. They are selling financial products, either some sort of insurance-based product like life or disability insurance, or some type of investment product such as stocks, bonds, or mutual funds, for the purpose of filling a need. In many cases they are sold with a tax-favored system involved. However, in most cases these products are sold without much regard for how they integrate with one another in a comprehensive financial plan.

So what is a comprehensive financial plan? Here's my definition: a comprehensive financial plan is a systematic approach toward integrating all aspects of a person's financial life for the purpose of improving their financial well-being both today and in the future. It includes planning for the accumulation, use and distribution of wealth. Developing a comprehensive financial plan includes a holistic approach to determining your core values and establishing written goals that are compatible with those values.

The planning process includes an assessment of all aspects of your current financial situation, including a detailed assessment of ALL assets and liabilities and a detailed analysis of your personal cash flow. A financial plan includes a written implementation plan designed to maximize the likelihood of achieving your prioritized financial goals. A comprehensive plan will include a review, an analysis, and a systematic implementation process that will coordinate all financial areas of your life. At minimum the financial topics listed below will be included when designing a written plan:

1. Personal cash management
2. Debt management, debt reduction & debt elimination
3. Insurance: Life, health, disability, property & casualty (auto, home, etc.), mal-practice, business, long-term care, umbrella coverage, etc.
4. Employee benefit plans

5. Income taxes
6. Business structure, i.e. sole proprietor, C Corp, S Corp, LLC
7. Asset accumulation
   a. Short-term savings
   b. Retirement planning
   c. Educational funding
8. Investment analysis
9. Estate planning considerations
   a. Estate distribution (gifting, wills, trusts, etc,)
   b. Estate taxes
   c. Other legal documents: general and medical powers of attorney, etc.

There are many objectives in comprehensive financial planning. Here are a few:

1. Identifying those things that are most important to you.
2. Establishing and prioritizing financial goals.
3. Determining what can be done now to improve your immediate financial situation, i.e. personal cash flow, reducing debt, reducing taxes, eliminating unnecessary expenses.
4. Minimizing costly mistakes, i.e. avoid purchasing costly insurance and/or investment vehicles that are not maximizing your chances of meeting your goals.
5. Developing the best strategies of accumulating wealth, using wealth assets during your life, and ultimately the distribution of wealth at death.

So let's get started!

Practicing Good Financial Hygiene

What do you think is the number-one cause of periodontal disease? It's poor dental hygiene, right? That makes sense to me. That would include not brushing regularly, not flossing, not going to the dentist for regular checkups and routine cleanings. Would you agree? These are the basics of dental hygiene. When basic dental hygiene is not followed, then it goes without saying that serious dental problems are sure to arise. Problems associated with periodontal disease such as cavities, broken teeth, and tooth loss, are likely to occur, and it's possible that other serious systemic health issues could arise. So what's the best medicine to prevent all this? I'm sure you would agree that prevention is the best medicine in battling periodontal disease. How long does it actually take to brush your teeth? Two minutes? It's amazing, two minutes a couple of times a day for brushing your teeth, coupled with flossing once a day and seeing your dentist twice a year, can help you to keep your teeth for the rest of your life.

Prevention and planning are important to financial health as well. What, you don't have the time? Why is it so important to plan anyway? You might be saying, "I'll start planning when I get out of debt, or perhaps I'll start planning when I'm making some real money, or when I get married or after we have children." Well, what if I was to say to you, "I'll start brushing my child's teeth when all of them come in. Why even bother? They are only his baby teeth, they're going to fall out anyway. I'll start brushing them after the permanent teeth come in. I'll start taking care of them then."

Your response might sound like this, "Well, by starting early you'll teach your child good dental hygiene habits. These good habits will be carried with him throughout life and will very likely help him to keep his teeth and enjoy a healthy smile for the rest of his life." I'm sure you are getting my point with this illustration. Just as poor dental hygiene can lead to serious dental problems, poor financial hygiene can lead to a slew of financial problems, such as debt (personal and professional), income tax problems, cash flow issues, credit trouble, stress, relationship problems and even physical ailments.

Establishing good habits early is key.

So we agree, good dental hygiene needs to be taught at an early age, and establishing good financial habits early on is essential for your personal long-term financial health.

As a dental professional you know the benefits of good dental hygiene. Good financial hygiene has many benefits as well. Good financial hygiene helps you:
  a. Identify those things that you value most in life.
  b. Avoid costly financial mistakes
  c. Make smart choices with your money
  d. Simplify your financial decisions
  e. Improve your cash flow
  f. Simplify your life
  g. Protect yourself against risks of financial loss
  h. Maximize your wealth potential
  i. Improve your personal relationships

The truth is though, most people have never been taught good financial hygiene habits. I have found that regardless of their level of education, many people don't know the basics of personal financial management. Good financial hygiene habits are not taught by a lot of parents and definitely are not included in most school curriculum. Although many people learn to make money, most people are not taught how to manage this money.

Well, it's never too late to start good dental hygiene, and it's never too late to start practicing good financial hygiene. Good financial hygiene includes the following:
  1. Starting Early – This includes saving money, paying yourself first and developing a comprehensive financial plan.
  2. Identifying those things that you value most in life.
  3. Setting goals that are compatible with your values.

4. Living within or below your income.
5. Avoiding consumer debt.
6. Taking advantage of the wisdom of trusted advisors, i.e. your CPA, attorney and your Certified Financial Planner™ professional.
7. Having regular financial checkups. Being accountable to someone other than yourself regarding your finances.

Remember, I'm here to help you.

The remainder of this book is devoted to helping you implement and continue the process of good financial hygiene. Regardless of where you are right now, whether you're just getting started in practice as an employee, starting your own practice, been in practice for several years, or are looking to retire in the near future, the information in this book will help you. How? First of all, it will let you identify the things that are most important to you – those things you value most. It will help you avoid costly financial mistakes that I have witnessed made by many dental professionals. This book will help you make smart choices with your money. It will help you simplify your financial decisions, show you how to streamline your financial life, allow you to identify and protect yourself against risks of financial loss, and ultimately lead you toward maximizing your wealth potential. And I believe it will even improve your personal relationships with others. Regardless of where you stand right now, this book will help you *Bridge the Gap* in your personal finances.

Values

Is making smart choices about your money important to you? "Well, isn't it to everyone?" you might respond! You hear a lot about the word *values* today. Sometimes when you hear a word a lot, you tend to put less thought into its meaning or importance. For our purpose here, I believe it is important to define what I mean by values. In this context, values are defined as the beliefs and ideas that are most important to you! In his book, *Values-Based Financial Planning*, Bill Bachrach says, "Values are those qualities and principles that are intrinsically valuable to you. In other words, they are life's emotional payoffs." Values define the things that are most important in life to you and they are the underlying reason(s) you make the decisions you make.

So many of us move through life just going from one day to the next, without even knowing why we are doing what we do. We know we should save for retirement, we know we should save for college for our kids. But we don't ever seem to get around to it. We know that we shouldn't put that new blouse on the credit card or borrow the money to buy that boat, but we do it anyway. We know it would be wise to wait to buy a bigger house or a new car. But we don't want to wait. We want it now and we do it now because, in that particular moment, it makes us feel good. Rather than thinking through a financial decision, we make our decision based upon what it will do for us today, right now!

So why do so many people make decisions this way? I believe it is because most people have never sat down to explore what's really important to them. They don't really know what they value in life. Oh, they may know how important it is to them to spend time with their family and friends. And they may know that they value honesty and integrity and hard work. But they have never sat down and listed out those things that are really important (valuable) to them and then aligned their financial decisions with those things that they value most. Let's take a minute to stop and think.

Here's a question for you. *"What's important about money to you?"*

Is it that money provides you security? Okay, then what's important about security to you? Is it that having security and knowing that the bills are paid gives you peace of mind? Great! What's important about having that peace of mind to you? Wow, that's a tough one isn't it? What's important about peace of mind to you? Hey I know, "When I have peace of mind, I'm more relaxed and not so stressed out." Terrific! Tell me what's important to you about not being stressed out? "Well, when I'm not stressed out I feel better about who I am; I feel like I actually have a life and that I'm not just going from one day to the next without really knowing why. I feel as though I am actually living up to my full potential." So, what's important about living up to your full potential? Well, when I am living up to my full potential I feel that I am actually adding something to society and making a difference in the lives of others. In other words I feel like I am fulfilling my purpose in life and truly living a life of value!"

As you can see this process of determining *what you value most in life* is much more than just goal setting. So how will identifying what is most important to you help you bridge the financial gap? First, this exercise is designed to help you identify what is really most important to you in life. Identifying your values will help inspire you to achieve the goals you set for yourself. Your values are your emotional payoff! Your values are the reasons behind your goals. Your values are what will inspire you to achieve your goals. In the Olympic games, the gold medal may be the prize, but it is the emotional feeling of great achievement that is the real payoff. Does this make sense? I hope so.

One of the most important things in life to me is being able to spend time with my wife, Rhonda, and my three boys, Trent, Jared and Cameron. Yes, I believe quality time is important, but I believe in quantity time as well. When I think that my kids spend nearly 10 hours a day during the school week away from me, then another 8 to 10 hours sleeping, it really bothers me. And though there's not much I can do about it, I can control how much time I am able to spend with them when they are awake and aren't in school.

For instance, the last week of May is always an exciting time around our house. Why? Because the kids are out of school, that's why. Why am I so excited about my kids getting out of school? After all, the Staples' commercial says "the most wonderful time of the year" is when the kids are going back to school. I disagree. Why?

Fridays! Fridays are why I am so excited. From the first Friday to the last Friday of summer vacation I'll tell you exactly where we'll be as a family. Lake Pleasant. Why do we go on Fridays? Because on Fridays there are no weekend crowds. Instead there's nothing but smooth water and lots of room for us to enjoy ourselves. So while others are at work, we are out enjoying quality family time. There's nothing better than making the first wake on the smoothness of the glass-like lake water. A MasterCard® commercial might say it like this: "An ice chest full of cold drinks - $25, a full tank of gas – $75, custom wakeboard boots – $300, watching your son land his first flip on his new wake board? Priceless!"

I'm not sharing this with you to impress you. If you're not already enjoying the lifestyle of a three- or four-day workweek you probably will (if you choose to) someday. I tell you this in order to show you something that is very valuable to me, spending Friday on the lake with my wife and kids. I know that by investing quality and quantity time with my family that I will have more opportunity to positively impact the people I care about most. That is really what is important to me in life. After all, if life were just about making more money I would be working every Friday.

Perhaps there are similar things that are valuable to you. Ask yourself these questions, "What are the things that are the most important in life to me? What do I really value in life? Am I working just for the sake of creating wealth?" You might be, but I doubt it. Wealth for wealth sake is really pretty meaningless. It's what you do with that wealth that really makes the difference. We've all seen examples of people who have tremendous wealth but at the same time their personal lives are a shambles. You know what I am talking about. If you need an illustration of what I am talking about, just watch an episode of *Entertainment Tonight*.

Roy Disney once said, "When your values are clear, your decisions are easy." I urge you to take the time to uncover and list those things that you value most. Once you do, then work to center your financial decisions based upon the things on that list. You will be amazed how easy your decision process will become.

Below is a brief email conversation I had with a dental hygienist. It is another example of what I am talking about.

Dear Larry,

Thank you SO much for your time and honesty in our conversation yesterday. You certainly have a sixth sense when talking to your clients. One last question for you...where do I draw the line in returning back to work to buy "things" or to be more "stable?" It seems to me I am going back for all the wrong reasons. I feel as if I am chasing after what matters in the world, yet new furniture would be great! I am a dental hygienist and a personal trainer. I teach two classes per week. It is just blow money...not that much.

I would greatly appreciate your opinion. I won't hold you to anything! Email me at your convenience. I know you are very busy...I just see someone who has a lot of wisdom to offer. You certainly have chosen a great profession for yourself.

Thanks again for your time. I really appreciate it, Larry.

Karen

Dear Karen,

This may seem like a tough question. However, it's pretty simple. What are the things that are most important to you? Chasing the things of the world is a challenge we all face every day. But you need to ask yourself why you would be going back to work? By the way, I don't think there is anything wrong with returning to work (even to improve your lifestyle). The challenge is to not take it to a level where you then LOCK YOURSELF into that lifestyle by creating higher FIXED expenses (i.e., bigger house, higher car payments, etc.). Also, you have to consider how it will affect your family (i.e. not being home when the kids come home from school).

Interestingly enough, this past week my wife and I were looking at purchasing a larger home in a more prestigious neighborhood. It was a great house and we could afford it, but after our three sons and saw the house, we decided we didn't want to move out of our spacious cul-de-sac. After all, their friends were there and we would be giving up our baseball field (the cul-de-sac). We had to re-evaluate our reasons for wanting to move. When we did, we decided to stay where we were.

It comes down to knowing what is most important to you. I would be happy to sit down with you and Tom and take you through an exercise that will help you in this area. "When your values are clear, your decisions are easy." (Roy Disney.)

Sincerely,
Larry

Let me share one more real life story with you. I have a husband and wife client that I have worked with as their financial advisor for several years. But it was only within the last two years that I walked them through this value discovery process. About a year ago, they called me while they were vacationing in Hawaii. They told me how they sat through a timeshare presentation and they got very excited about buying a timeshare in Maui. (Imagine that!)

I said to them, "Wow, that sounds great. I'm sure you can afford it. Tell me how this timeshare fits into what's most important to you in your life?" Well, it was quiet on the other end of the phone, so I reminded them of how they wanted to be free from debt and how important it was to reduce the time they spend working in their practice from four days a week to three days a week. I reminded them how they had shared with me what they really wanted was to be free from debt and the stress that it was causing in their lives; and how important it was to them to be able to spend more time together as a family.

But they were excited about this timeshare. Well, who wouldn't be excited about having a timeshare in Hawaii? I know I would. The truth is, they could have written a check and felt good about it, for now anyway. It probably would not have affected their lifestyle that much. However, after a short three-minute discussion they knew that the decision to buy this timeshare did not fit with those things that were most important to them.

That was it; they had made their decision and it wasn't that difficult. All they needed was to clarify their values and once they did, their decision was easy. By the way, I didn't tell them NO. That's not my job; after all it's their money, not mine. I simply helped them clarify their values. They had a plan and were willing to stick to it because they knew what was most important to them.

Setting Goals

Once you have a clear vision of what's really important to you, then and only then should you begin to set your goals. As values are our intangible desires, goals are the tangible things we desire. Goals are personal milestones such as: financial independence, owning a vacation home, sending your children to college, being debt free, and traveling around the world. So what's involved in setting goals?

Before we discuss the process of goal setting, imagine this scenario. You're sitting on an airplane with the intention of flying from Los Angeles to New York. As you're sitting there waiting to take off, the pilot comes on the intercom. "Good morning ladies and gentlemen, this is your captain speaking. Thank you for flying with us today. We should get around to taking off sometime today, and when we do we're going to fly around for a while. I'm not exactly sure where we're going and I'm not sure how much fuel we have. But we're going to take off and hopefully we'll find a runway somewhere to land this crate. So buckle up and hold on, it should be an exciting ride!"

Tell me, how long would it take for you to get off that plane? I'm sure you would be off that plane as fast I would. You would probably prefer to hear something like this instead. "Good morning ladies and gentleman, this is your captain speaking. We're number two in line for takeoff. We will be departing at 7:17 this morning for our flight to New York's LaGuardia Airport. Our flight time will be 4 hours and 47 minutes. We will be flying at 33,000 feet. Currently it's cool and rainy in New York, but it should warm up to 65 degrees with clear skies by the time we land at 3:04 pm New York time. We are expecting a smooth ride, but please keep your seatbelt fastened while seated. Please sit back and relax, and we'll keep you posted on our progress throughout the flight. Again, thank you for flying with us."

Though most people would prefer to fly with the second captain, many people tend to go about setting financial goals in the same style of the first pilot. Many people seem to say to themselves; "I don't really know what I want to accomplish financially, but I'm going to do my best to make some money, enjoy my life and hopefully things will all work out in the end."

Setting Successful Goals

In his book *Smart Women Finish Rich*, David Bach says, "When setting goals you need to make them S.M.A.C." Goals need to be Specific, Measurable, Achievable and Compatible. Let's explore each of these separately.

Specific – "I want to pay off my house," is not a specific goal. Here is an example of a specific goal. "I want to have my mortgage loan of $278,500 paid off by March 15, 2018." This goal says exactly what is to be accomplished; that is to pay off a specific amount of debt ($278,500) by a specific point in time (March 15, 2018).

Measurable – The above goal is also measurable. It is measured by both the amount of the loan and the date by which it is to be paid in full. With a measurable goal you can monitor your progress toward your goal, and you will know when the goal has been met.

Achievable – It is vital that your goals be realistically achievable. A goal to retire by age 55 with an after-tax monthly income of $5,000 may or may not be achievable. It depends, are you 53 years old now and have nothing in savings? Well, unless you have a rich uncle who is on his deathbed who plans on leaving you a small fortune, then it's probably not realistic.

However, if you are 35 years old, have your debt under control and are maximizing your retirement plan contributions, then you will have a much better chance of achieving your goal.

The fact is if your goal is not realistic (achievable) then you will soon give up on it once reality sets in. When establishing achievable financial goals ask yourself these questions:
  1. What do I have saved (how much money) to help me achieve this goal?
  2. How much time do I have to reach the goal?

3. What future resources (i.e., from income) can I allocate to this
   goal?

Your answers to these questions will help you determine if your goal is
achievable.

Compatible – Finally, your goals must also be compatible. Compatible
with what? Your goals must be compatible with your values (those
things that are most important to you)!

If you want to be totally debt free by, let's say April 30, 2022, and that
includes all debt including your mortgage, how do you think buying a
timeshare in Hawaii would fit in to your plan? Well, that depends. Can
you have it paid for by April 30, 2022, without compromising your
values as well as other financial goals? If so, okay. If not, well then you
should probably not purchase the timeshare.

Don't miss this next point. *It is essential that you put your goals in
writing.* By writing your goals down, you have taken them from what I
refer to as wishful hopes or dreams, to goals. Here's an example that will
illustrate the value of writing out your goals. Have you ever watched
college basketball? If you have, you have probably seen something like
this. There are 2.6 seconds left on the clock. The team is down by 2
points. The coach knows if he wants to win, they will need to make a
three pointer. Does the coach just say; "Let's just throw the ball in to
somebody, throw it up and hope it goes in?" No way! What is it they
almost always do? They have a whiteboard (or large notepad) and they
draw out (they write out) their plan for the team to see. The coach makes
sure that every player knows exactly where they need to be and they
know who is going to get the ball. And when the winning basket is
scored, it happens because this is not just a wishful hope; but this is a
written goal, planned out with specific intention and with measurable
and achievable results with the right players and talent to score the
basket. And this is exactly how you need to approach your personal goal
setting.

Okay, so you have written out your Specific, Measurable, Achievable and
Compatible goals. You're done right? Not yet. There's one more step in
the goal setting process. After you have set your goal, describe to yourself
in two or three words how you will feel when you achieve them. Let me

illustrate what I mean. Fill in the sentences below with your personal criteria.

"I want to be financially independent by age _____ with an after-tax monthly income of $_____." (Insert your own age and desired income.) Okay, now you are _____ years old and have a monthly retirement income of $_____, and you have the choice as to whether or not you go to work. Close your eyes and really try hard to put yourself there. Now, give me two or three words that describe how you are feeling once you are there. Do any of these come to mind? Excited! Psyched! Overjoyed! Happy as can be! Relieved! Free! I hope so.

As you set your goals, it is essential that you repeat this process for each new goal or milestone. It is this process that will help you to achieve your goals in life and ultimately help you to live a life centered on those things that are most important to you. The process will not only help you to live your life based upon your values, but also help you to live a life of value.

Another important point. I highly recommend you share your goals with someone you trust. This person should be someone who could ultimately help you achieve your goal or someone who has a vested interest in helping you achieve your goal. It could be your spouse, a financial planner, a family member, a close friend, or a business partner; but it should be someone who will be a positive influence in helping you reach your goals.

Although this book focuses on financial matters, I am confident that this goal setting process will help you in other areas of your life as well. I personally set goals using this same process in many different areas of my own life. I share my financial goals with my own advisors, my family, as well as some of my clients. I also have goals to continue to improve my personal relationships with my wife and children and I have mentors who I share these personal goals with. I apply these same principles to my spiritual and physical goals as well. Sharing your goals with someone else and becoming accountable outside yourself can be of tremendous value in helping you reach whatever type of goals you have.

Know Where You Stand Financially

Cash, Assets, Debts and Insurance

Once you know what is most important to you and you have put your goals in writing, you need to determine where you stand financially. The first step is to *find your stuff!* (I got this great line from David Bach.) I know everyone has different organizational skills. You may know exactly where all your paperwork stuff is, or you may have stuff at the office and stuff at home. You may have stuff under the filing cabinet, in the filing cabinet and on top of the filing cabinet. You may have stuff in the credenza and stuff underneath the bed. You may have stuff in the garage and even stuff in the car. Wherever it is, you need to find it, because until you know where you stand financially, you can't even begin working toward your goals.

Below is a Financial Documents Checklist that will help you know what stuff you are looking for. You can also access an updated copy of this list at www.BridgingTheFinancialGap.com.

Financial Document Checklist

Risk Management
- Life insurance policies, latest statements, and loan data
- Disability insurance policies
- Medical and long term care insurance policies
- Auto, home, professional liability, malpractice, business & umbrella Insurance

Savings
- Savings account and certificate of deposit statements
- Money market/cash management accounts

Debt Management
- Latest credit card statements
- Outstanding balances on all auto loans
- Mortgage balance: years remaining and interest rate
- Information on all other debts, 2nd mortgages, business loans, etc.

Investment Planning
- Investment documents, correspondence, prospectuses
- Latest statements from retirement plans and brokerage accounts
- Real estate investment purchase, escrow, and loan documents
- Investment partnership agreements

Tax Planning
- Tax returns for the last 2 years
- Recent payroll statements

Retirement Planning
- Latest statements from IRA, Keogh and other qualified retirement plans
- Employee benefits/retirement plan summaries and latest statement
- Deferred compensation and stock option agreements
- Pension/profit sharing plans
- Annuity policies and latest statements
- Social Security benefits summary statement

Estate Planning
- Wills
- Living wills
- Powers of attorney
- Trust documents

Corporate/Business Documents
- Corporate tax returns for the last 2 years
- Current profit & loss statement
- Current balance sheet
- Partnership/shareholder agreements
- Buy/sell agreements

Once you have everything together, you can then begin to prepare your personal financial statements. There are two personal financial statements you will want to prepare: your personal balance sheet and your personal cash flow statement. The purpose of these statements is twofold. First, the personal balance sheet will give you a "picture" of where you stand financially right now. That is, it will show you what the value of your assets are, and how much debt you have at a particular point in time. Secondly, your Personal Cash Flow Statement will show you where your money is going, in other words what you are spending your income on. I want to stress to you that the preparation of these two financial statements is vitally important, as they will form the foundation of your financial plan. In addition, it is important that you update your financial statements regularly. Think of updating these documents like periodontal charting, as they will provide you with an easy measurement as to whether your financial health is improving or getting worse.

Let's start by preparing your personal balance sheet. In order to complete your personal balance sheet there are two worksheets you will want to complete first. The first is the list of assets spreadsheet and the second is the schedule of debts spreadsheet. Both of these worksheets will be useful when preparing your personal balance sheet. You can get copies of these worksheets online at www.BridgingTheFinancialGap.com. Once you have completed both of these forms, you can then transfer the information over to your personal balance sheet. A blank balance sheet as well as a sample balance sheet can also be found at www.BridgingTheFinancialGap.com.

The List of Assets on your balance sheet should include the following four asset categories:
   USE ASSETS: Such as your home, cars, furnishings, etc.
   CASH RESERVES: Such as checking accounts, savings accounts, money funds, CDs, etc. Both personal and business accounts should be listed.
   GROWTH ASSETS: Such as stocks, bonds, mutual funds, IRAs, 401(k) Plans, real estate, value of your practice, etc.
   OTHER ASSETS: Cash value life insurance, collectibles, etc.

In addition to your assets you will also list all of your debts (taken from your schedule of debts spreadsheet) on your personal balance sheet. See the example balance sheet provided.

Personal Balance Sheet

USE ASSETS	$ VALUE	PERSONAL LIABILITIES		
Residence	$ 800,000	Residence	$	380,000
Auto #1	20,000			
Auto #2	15,000			
Other Use Assets	12,000	TOTAL PERSONAL		
TOTAL USE ASSETS	$ 847,000	LIABILITIES	$	380,000
CASH RESERVES				
Savings	$ 12,000			
Money Market	15,000			
Checking	10,000			
Business Savings	40,000			
TOTAL CASH RESERVES	$ 77,000			
GROWTH ASSETS				
IRAs, 401(k), Other Retirement	$ 243,000			
Stocks, Bonds, Mutual Funds	78,300	BUSINESS LIABILITIES		
Dental Building	660,000	Dental Building	$	280,000
TOTAL GROWTH ASSETS	$ 981,300			
OTHER ASSETS				
Cash Value Life Insurance	$ 0			
Collectibles	$ 0			
Others	$ 0			
Total Other Assets	$ 0	TOTAL LIABILITIES	$	660,000
TOTAL ALL ASSETS	$2,148,300	NET WORTH		$ 1,488,300

The next financial statement you need to put together is your personal cash flow statement. Developing the personal cash flow statement can often be difficult for some people. The reason it can be difficult is that many people do not really know where their money is going. (The truth is most people don't even know what their income is.) If you're one of those people who don't have a good handle on where your money is going (and have too much month at the end of the money) I strongly suggest you begin to track all of your expenses. The easiest way to do this is to write down all of your expenses for the next 30 days. You should include everything from your regular monthly expenses like your mortgage, utilities, car payments, as well as all of your cash purchases. Here are a couple of important points. First, you will need to write down everything. Secondly, try not to change your buying patterns. Often when people undertake this exercise they tend not to make purchases they normally would, so be careful not to change your buying habits (especially those impulse purchases) so you will have an accurate portrait of your expenses.

One way of tracking your cash expenditures is to carry a small notepad with you at all times. This may seem tedious, but believe me, after 30 days you will have a very good understanding of where your money is going.

Below is an expense summary worksheet that includes many common expense items. Completing this worksheet will help you determine your personal expenses and help you complete your personal cash flow Statement. You can also download this worksheet in the "Resources" section at www.BridgingTheFinancialGap.com.

Personal Cash Flow Worksheet

	MONTHLY	OR NON-MONTHLY
SAVINGS		
Retirement (401k, IRA, PSP, etc.)	$_____	$_____
Regular Savings (Bank/Money Mkt.)	$_____	$_____
TOTAL	$_____	$_____
HOUSING		
Mortgage (P, T, I)	$_____	$_____
Mortgage #2	$_____	$_____
Homeowner's/Renter's Insurance	$_____	$_____
Electric	$_____	$_____
Water	$_____	$_____
Gas	$_____	$_____
Phone	$_____	$_____
Cell Phone(s)/Pager(s)	$_____	$_____
Cable	$_____	$_____
Internet	$_____	$_____
Security Svc	$_____	$_____
Pool/Lawn Svc	$_____	$_____
Maintenance, Repairs, etc.	$_____	$_____
Association Dues	$_____	$_____

Cleaning Service $_____ $_____
TOTAL $_____ $_____

INSURANCE
Life Insurance $_____ $_____
Disability Insurance $_____ $_____
Long-Term Care Insurance $_____ $_____
Liability/(Umbrella Policy) $_____ $_____
TOTAL $_____ $_____

TRANSPORTATION
Payment/Lease #1 $_____ $_____
Payment/Lease #2 $_____ $_____
Gas $_____ $_____
Repairs/Maintenance $_____ $_____
Insurance $_____ $_____
TOTAL $_____ $_____

GROCERIES
Groceries at home $_____ $_____
Eating Out $_____ $_____
School Lunches $_____ $_____
TOTAL $_____ $_____

CLOTHING $_____ $_____

FURNISHINGS
Anticipated Purchases $_____ $_____

PERSONAL CARE
Dry Cleaning $_____ $_____
Salon $_____ $_____
Barber $_____ $_____
Gym $_____ $_____
TOTAL $_____ $_____

MEDICAL/DENTAL
Insurance Premiums $_____ $_____
Dental/Orthodontist $_____ $_____
Prescriptions $_____ $_____

Co-pays/Physician/Chiropractor	$_____	$_____
TOTAL	$_____	$_____

EDUCATION $_____ $_____

DEBT PAYMENTS
(Itemize credit cards and store debt below) $_____ $_____

ENTERTAINMENT
Dining Out, Movies, Etc. $_____ $_____
Kids – (sports, dance, music lessons, etc.) $_____ $_____

CHILD CARE/BABY SITTING $_____ $_____

HOLIDAYS/GIFTS
Birthdays $_____ $_____
Christmas/Hanukkah, etc. $_____ $_____
TOTAL $_____ $_____

VACATIONS/TRAVEL $_____ $_____

CHARITABLE GIVING $_____ $_____

TOTAL EXPENSES $_____ $_____

OTHER EXPENSES
Alimony/Child Support $_____ $_____
Magazines, Newspaper, etc. $_____ $_____
TOTAL $_____ $_____

Credit Card or Other Debt	Min Payment	Interest Rate	Balance Owed
_____	$_____	_____%	$_____
_____	$_____	_____%	$_____
_____	$_____	_____%	$_____
_____	$_____	_____%	$_____

After you have completed the expense worksheet you can then begin to prepare your personal cash flow statement. Your cash flow statement should include all income sources as well as all of your expenses. Refer to the sample cash flow statement to see how this financial statement

Sample Cash Flow Statement

	Annual Amount	Monthly Average	Percent of Total Income
INCOME			
Salary (Dr. Sample)	$ 120,000.00	$ 10,000.00	57%
"S Corp" Distributions	$ 87,000.00	$ 7,250.00	41%
Interest & Dividends	$ 2,970.00	$ 247.50	1%
Total Income	$ 209,970.00	$ 17,497.50	100%
DISBURSEMENTS			
Savings			
401(k)	$ 15,000.00	$ 1,250.00	7%
Regular Savings	$ 5,000.00	$ 416.67	2%
NQ Mutual Funds	$ 6,000.00	$ 500.00	3%
Total Savings	$ 26,000.00	$ 2,166.67	12%
Taxes			
Federal Taxes	$ 33,240.00	$ 2,770.00	16%
State Income Taxes	$ 5,715.00	$ 476.25	3%
OASDI/Medicare	$ 8,147.00	$ 678.92	4%
Total Taxes	$ 47,102.00	$ 3,925.17	22%
Expenses			
Housing	$ 66,280.00	$ 5,523.33	32%
Insurance	$ 11,990.00	$ 999.17	6%
Transportation	$ 17,443.00	$ 1,453.58	8%
Groceries	$ 10,200.00	$ 850.00	5%
Dining/Entertainment	$ 7,800.00	$ 650.00	4%
Personal Care	$ 2,780.00	$ 231.67	1%
Medical/Dental Expenses	$ 2,260.00	$ 188.33	1%
Debt Payments	$ 5,335.00	$ 444.58	3%
Child Care	$ 855.00	$ 71.25	0%
Vacations	$ 5,000.00	$ 416.67	2%
Charitable Giving	$ 4,200.00	$ 350.00	2%
Total Expenses	$ 134,143.00	$ 11,178.58	64%
Total Disbursements	$ 207,245.00	$ 17,270.42	99%
SURPLUS	$ 2,725.00	$ 227.08	1%

*Percentages differ slightly due to rounding.

should look when it is completed. As you review your personal cash flow statement, you will soon figure out whether you are living below, living within, or living above your income. If you are living above your income you are also most likely going into debt as you are finding yourself with too much month at the end of the money. We'll talk more about how to approach this challenge soon.

Emergency Reserves

Before moving on to cash management, I want to discuss the need to have an emergency reserve. After completing the expense worksheet this is a good time for you to determine how much money you should keep in your emergency reserve. Generally speaking you should keep six months of your fixed expenses in your emergency reserve account. Your fixed expenses are those expenses that you have to make: the house payment, utilities, and car payments. To assist you in this area the italicized expenses on the personal cash flow worksheet are what I consider to be fixed. Yours may be slightly different depending on your situation. Let's assume your fixed expenses total $7,000 per month. Then you should have an emergency reserve of $42,000.

This reserve should be held in a liquid account; such as a bank or credit union savings account, money market account or certificates of deposit.

Cash Management, Getting Out and Staying Out of Debt

This is it! This is the key to successful financial planning! This is the key to staying out of debt! This is the key to accumulating wealth! This is the key to reducing financial stress in your life. Are you ready? Great, here it is. Spend less money than you make! "That's it? Spend less money than I make? That's it?" "Come on," you might be saying, " there's got to be more to it than that." No, that's it. Spend less money than you make.

My father-in-law was a U.S. Steel worker for thirty years and he couldn't wait for the next layoff. Why? It was an extended vacation for him with partial pay. He would actually go out and pay cash for a brand new Chevy truck while he was laid off. How could he do that? It was simple. He saved money every working day of his life. And he lived below his income. At seventy-four years old today, he can pretty much do what he wants, and he retired at age fifty-five. This is a U.S. Steel worker, not a dentist, not a surgeon, but a U.S. Steel worker. How did he do that? He spent less money than he made.

My mother was no different. My mom was thirty-five years old when my father died. She had never worked outside the home, up to the time of my father's death. When my dad died, my mother became a single mother with seven children ranging from age 2 to 16 years old. She never remarried and when she retired in 1992 at age 62, she was debt free including her home and car. She had paid for two college educations (books and tuition); one of those was mine. On top of that she had accumulated a six-figure nest egg.

Here's the amazing thing. The year my mom retired was her highest income year and she made all of $22,667. And get this, she was self-employed so she had to pay both the employee and employer portions into Social Security. In addition, she even paid a seasonal employee out of that money, but even still she retired debt free at age 62. Now my father also had some life insurance, but mom was smart with that too. She didn't spend it; she found a good investment advisor, who helped her set up an income stream from the death benefit of the policy.

Living Within Your Income

So how is it that a steelworker could buy a new truck during a lay-off, and retire at age 55? And how is it that a single mother of seven retires debt free at age 62? Very simple, they lived within their income. They spent less money than they earned. Here it comes. Get ready! They lived on a budget. OUCH! I can hear it now. "A budget? You have got to be kidding! Do you know how much money I make? I don't need to live on a budget." Guess what? You're right; you don't have to live on a budget. You don't have to do anything. You can also continue to suffer from the stress of living beyond your means. However, let's discuss the benefits of living within your income, within a budget.

Before I get started about the value of utilizing a personal budget I want to make sure you understand something. I am a big believer that you should strive to enjoy your life. After all you didn't spend four or more years in college, another four years in dental school and maybe another two to five years beyond that if you are a specialist, to make a lot of money and *not enjoy it!* And as a dental practitioner you no doubt work hard! So yes, enjoy your life and have a good time. However, remember this famous proverb, *"It's okay to enjoy the fruits of your labor, but you don't have to eat every grape in the bowl."* By the way, if you have never heard this famous proverb, it's because I just made it up. Who knows, maybe *it will be* famous one day!

Telling people that they should learn to budget their income is like telling someone they need to go on a diet. Unfortunately, these two words have taken on a negative connotation in our society. To make the word diet sound better some refer to it as "an eating plan." To make the word budget sound better, many in my business will refer to it as Cash Flow Management or perhaps Lifestyle Spending. Well, if major corporations like Microsoft, Coca-Cola, and Wal-Mart, as well as hundreds of other companies can use the word budget, then so will I. There isn't a major corporation in America that operates without a budget. Why? Because if they don't plan their expenses in relation to their income, they are very likely to overspend and lose money. Then they may have to borrow money, causing them to become over extended, thus causing the value of their stock to drop. This in turn will make for a lot of very upset stockholders, who just happen to elect the board of directors!

So, why don't more people operate within a budget? I believe the biggest reason is because our society has been plagued by two very serious financial diseases—Stuffitis and Affluenza. Their symptoms are very similar to one another. When a person has become exposed to either of these social viruses they have an insatiable desire to have stuff and live a life of affluence, and even when they can't afford whatever it is they want, they buy it anyway. Usually on credit. They want it and they want it now! And in many cases they will do whatever it takes to get it, even if it means over extending themselves with debt. After all, it's just another monthly payment of $300 or $500 or $700.

I have found that after a dental professional has been in practice for a few years and they have the so-called trappings of success: the cars, houses, vacations, boats, second homes in the mountains. Many of them are too embarrassed to admit that they are living paycheck to paycheck just like the "average Joe." They're buried in debt and have very little money in the bank, much less in a retirement plan. They say to themselves, "When I get this credit card debt paid off, or the build-out loan paid off, then I will start socking some money away." That is, until the guy down the road comes by and tells them about this great new piece of equipment or shows off his new Cadillac Escalade.

I'm not slamming the dental profession here. I'm just telling it like it is for most people in our society. I'm not saying that we should hoard every dollar and live without nice things. That's why we became educated in the first place – to get ahead, enjoy life, enjoy time off, and have nice things. However, like I said earlier, "it's okay to enjoy the fruits of your labor, but you don't have to eat every grape in the bowl!"

People don't understand the value of a budget.
Many people don't understand the real purpose or value of having a budget. What is the purpose of a budget? The purpose of a budget is to give you permission to spend a planned amount of money in various areas of your financial life, not just to keep you from spending money. A budget lays out the ground rules for where your income will go. A budget helps

you reduce what I refer to as reactionary spending. Reactionary spending occurs when expenses come up that are not planned or prepared for. Reactionary spending occurs in many different forms. It can occur when the air-conditioning goes out, when you decide on a whim to take a weekend trip or when you're just shopping at Costco.

A budget tells you what your fixed expenses are; such as your income taxes, property taxes, house payment, auto expenses, groceries, utilities, etc. It tells you how much of your income goes toward debt reduction, short-term savings and retirement savings. Furthermore the purpose of a budget is to help plan your discretionary spending for things like vacations, entertainment, or dining out. And last, but not least, the purpose of a budget is to keep you from overspending and GOING INTO DEBT!

Think of a budget like the lines on a highway or freeway. The lines are there to keep you safe and out of danger. Can you imagine driving on a Los Angeles freeway that doesn't have any lines between the lanes? Even the cars that are all headed in the same direction are going to be in trouble, someone is eventually going to get hurt or even killed. The lines on the roadways help keep you safe (well safer, anyway). A budget is no different. The purpose of a budget is to keep you safe *financially*. A budget can reduce your financial stress. It won't necessarily take away your desire for more. But it will keep you from *having* to make more money in order to pay for a lifestyle you can't really afford.

Here's another example. What is the value of knowing how much gasoline there is in your car? Well, that's pretty easy. If you don't know how much gas you have, how can you know how far you can drive without having to stop for gas? Can you imagine going on a long road trip or for that matter driving to the office in the morning without knowing whether or not you have enough gas in your car to get where you want to go? You're probably thinking, "That would be crazy. I wouldn't dream of going on a trip without knowing how much gas is in my tank and how far a tank of gas will take me." But that is exactly how millions of people operate their checkbooks everyday. Spend today, without knowing that they're running on empty.

I can't tell you how many people don't even know how much money they make, much less how much they spend and what they pay in income taxes! How about you, do you know what your gross annual income (after business expenses) is? Do you know what your personal monthly expenses are? What did you pay in income taxes last year? Not how much did you write a check for when you sent in your tax return. What was your actual tax bill? If you don't know, look at your Federal Tax Return (Form 1040) where it says, "This is your Total Tax."

Take it to Action - Write it Down!
Here's an exercise for you. Write down how much you think you spend monthly (after taxes) at home. Go ahead, think about it for a minute or two and then write it down. Now, complete the Summary of Expenses worksheet and compare your total to the number you wrote down. How close where you? If you are within 10%, then you probably have a very good handle on where your money is going (or maybe you just made a lucky guess.)

The point I am making here is pretty basic. You need to know what your income is and plan your expenses according to your income. Think about it this way. If you make $100,000 per year, then you earn $100,000 per year. Not $105,000. If you make $350,000 per year, then it's $350,000, not $360,000. If you don't know what it is, take a look at last year's tax return. Find the line on page 2 that shows total income. Look closely at this amount. This IS your income. Memorize this number, think about it, divide it by 12 (months) or 52 (weeks) or even by 365 (days) to figure out how much income you have available monthly, weekly or daily. The important thing is to come to terms with your true income and plan from there. Got it? Great!

How do you develop a spending plan or a budget?
First of all, you need to determine where your money is going. If you haven't already completed it, go back and complete the expense summary worksheet. Be sure to include those expenses that you may not be paying monthly; such as medical expenses, insurance, gifts and unexpected "emergency expenses," like home and auto repairs. It is vital to be as accurate as possible. Be sure to include taxes as well, this includes Federal, State and FICA taxes. These numbers can be found on your personal income tax returns and W2 or you can get these figures from your CPA.

Now you will need to compare your total expenses to your earned income. You should strive to account for 95% of your income to expenses. At this point you will be able to determine whether or not you are living within your means; more specifically, within your income amount. If your income is less than your expenses then at this point it will be necessary to adjust your spending patterns. This is not rocket science. If you are spending more than you are making, you will go into debt, and the farther you go, the more difficult it will become to get out.

If you determine that you're spending money you don't have and adjusting your spending becomes necessary, go back and re-examine those things that are most important to you. As you do this, also take a look at your expenses and then reduce or eliminate those expenses that aren't compatible with your values.

If you are a new dentist or if have been practicing for several years, do yourself a major favor. Don't let your lifestyle get ahead of your income! *In other words, don't let your lifestyle determine your need for income. That is, don't expand your lifestyle just because you're a doctor, or just because you "want" to live in a particular neighborhood.* Instead, be willing to sacrifice a little today to be able to create a life that you will enjoy for many, many years to come. I recently met a young orthodontic graduate who qualified for and purchased a $400,000 house and he doesn't even have a job yet! Don't let the lure of future earnings trap you into big debts early in your career. The price you pay may be a lot more than you think and I don't just mean financially.

I remember the first time I borrowed money.
My wife Rhonda and I got married in 1985 after we both graduated from Arizona State University. Within a month of getting married we moved to San Diego where I had accepted a sales position with the Ciba-Geigy Corporation, a large multi-national conglomerate, based in Basil, Switzerland.

I remember the day they offered me the job. It paid $22,600 per year and I thought I had made it. We were going to be on "Easy Street!" Well, after moving to San Diego, I quickly discovered there was *no such* street as Easy Street, at least not in San Diego, Calif. for someone earning $22,600 per year.

After renting a 700 square foot duplex at $550 per month for a year and a half, I got tired of flushing that rent money down the drain every month. So I said to my wife, "Rhonda, let's go out and look at houses. We need to buy a place of our own and stop wasting our money on rent!" Well, it took us less than two days to find the house of our dreams. It was 1,358 square feet with a nice yard for our two Basset hounds and lots of fruit trees. It really was a cute place. I wish I still owned it! The price was $100,500.

After talking with the realtor we determined that we could afford the payment if we could come up with a down payment of $20,000. We didn't want to pay for private mortgage insurance–PMI. So, "Who ya gonna call?" No, not ghost busters. Who else? Mom of course.

I remember calling my mom in Phoenix, Ariz. from our kitchen in Escondido, Calif. I called and said, "Hey mom, Rhonda and I just found this great house, it's only $100,500, but there's this thing called PMI (private mortgage insurance) and we need to put down $20,000 so we don't have to pay it." I then explained that Rhonda and I had saved $5,000, and we needed (wanted) to borrow $15,000 so that we would be able to buy the house.

Mom said, "Well I just sold some stock and I just happen to have the money available." Then she asked me to hold on. "Okay," I said. When she returned to the phone, she said, "Your payment will be $304.15, payable for the 60 months. I quickly did the math and said, "Mom, $304.15 a month for 60 months is more than $18,000." "That's right son, I'm charging you 8% interest." "Eight percent!" I said. Her response was quick and to the point, "I've been making 12 % on this money, do you want the loan or not?" "Okay, okay," I said, "Yes, I want the loan." We worked out some details and just before we hung up the phone, Mom said, "Your payment is due on the first of the month, by the way. And remember you live in California and it's going to take a couple of days to get here so be sure to mail it early enough to get it here by the first of the month." My only reply was, "Yes ma'am."

Well, we got the house and were living it up in our 1,358 square foot home in Escondido. About a year later, we wanted to buy a new vehicle. So we called Mom up. "Hey Mom, can we borrow five thousand dollars? We want to buy this truck, and..." Before I could finish my sentence, she said "No."

"Why, what's the deal?" I asked.

She said. "Larry, you're already late on your other payment to me. Why would I loan you anymore money with credit like yours?" I was devastated. Not because she said no, but because of why she said no. At that very moment I felt the bondage the debt had on me. To be honest it was humiliating. I was 24 years old and I did not like the feeling of bondage this debt had on me. Needless to say I immediately put together a game plan to pay my mother back the loan for the house. And I did, in full!

The point I'm making with this story is this; with debt comes bondage. Not physical bondage, but emotional bondage. Maybe you've felt this kind of bondage. It may not have been a loan from your mother or father, but maybe you have overextended your lifestyle and have excessive credit card debt or other consumer debt. Maybe you purchased an expensive car to treat yourself and realized later it wasn't really such a smart thing to do after all. Or perhaps you purchased more house than you really could afford (even though the mortgage company said you could). Whatever the reason, if you are in debt and have felt the bondage I am referring to then you may be asking yourself, what do I do now?

How to Get Out of Debt

The first thing you need to know is how much debt do you have? If you completed the earlier exercise and have prepared your personal balance sheet, then you already know how much debt you have. If you haven't completed this exercise then take the time to do it now.

Now that you know how much debt you have, the next thing you need to do is to put together a debt reduction/debt elimination plan. There are two basic methods of debt elimination. The first is to pay off the highest interest rate debt first and work your way down according to the interest rates you are paying. The second method includes paying off the smaller debts first and working your way to paying off the larger debts last. I tend to favor the latter mainly because it allows to you achieve some level of success sooner. It is this feeling of achievement that I believe will motivate you to continue on with your debt elimination plan.

The process of debt reduction/elimination is not going to be easy, but the reward(s) will be tremendous. If you are serious about getting out of debt you will need to go back and examine what you value most. For instance, if it is your desire to have a less stressful life so that you feel more secure, and therefore better able to enjoy your life with your family and others you care about, then working to rid yourself of debt will become a goal to allow you to achieve these values. Remember, it is the achievement (and the process of achievement) of your values that will lead you toward reaching your goals.

Though I believe that you should strive to pay off your personal home mortgage prior to retirement, the home mortgage should be (in most cases) one of the last debts to pay off due to the favorable tax treatment of mortgage interest. So for the purpose of this discussion we will assume that your home mortgage will be the last debt to be paid off.

Although I don't really believe in "good" debt, in this book I will classify debt as good debt and bad debt. You may have borrowed money to go to dental school, purchase your dental practice, purchase your office building or perhaps expand or update an existing practice. Yes, it would have been nice for someone to write a check for dental school or for your practice, but in most cases that just doesn't happen. So, I classify these as "good" debts. Another term for this type of debt is investment debt. This type of debt allows you to invest in building your practice. Here's an important point. Although I refer to investment debt, I want to be sure that you know that I do not recommend that you borrow money to purchase investments, like stocks, bonds or mutual funds or to fund an IRA or any other retirement plan.

Now that we have a good understanding of what good debt is, let me define "bad debt." Bad debt includes credit card debt, auto loans, boat and RV loans, and home equity lines of credit. When eliminating debt, the bad debt should be eliminated first. Here is an example of why: you have a credit card with a $5,000 balance, an interest rate of 18%, with a payment of $127. If you make this payment every month you will pay the credit card off in about 5 years (60 months). Your total payments will be $7,620. That includes $2,620 of interest over the 4-year period ($7,620 - $5,000 = $2,620) and that's on only a $5,000 debt. Let's say, however, you are able to pay an additional $100 per month against that $5,000 credit card. Your payment will be reduced to about 27 months, saving you $1,500 in interest.

In another example, let's look at a car loan of $50,000 with a 60-month payment plan and a 7% interest rate. Your monthly payment is $990.06

for 60 months, with total payments of $59,403.60 over the life of the loan. That's $9,403.60 in interest! If you increased your monthly payment by $500 you would pay the loan off in about 37.5 months, saving you nearly $3,600 in interest.

So what do you do if you don't have the income available to pay more than the minimum payment on your debt? Well, this is another good reason to know where your money is going. Once you see your true cash flow picture, then you can determine what expenses will need to be reduced or eliminated to provide additional cash toward debt elimination. Debt elimination is not a difficult science. In order to pay off debt quicker you will either have to increase your income and pay down debt with the increase or you will have to reduce expenses in several areas of your life.

David Bach, author of *Smart Women Finish Rich*, *Smart Couples Finish Rich* and the *Automatic Millionaire* describes what he calls the "Latte Factor.®" The premise of the Latte Factor is that we all have things that we spend money on that we don't really need, for example, lattes at nearly $4 each. A latte a day, five days a week is $20 per week for coffee! That's over $1,000 per year! Ten years ago, Americans wouldn't have dreamed of paying that for coffee, but for many people it's become part of their everyday life. David says that when you add a biscotti to the order the expense reaches over $1,500 per year!

Most of us have some sort of Latte Factor, for some it's coffee, for others it's eating out often, for others it may be clothes and for still others it's travel or entertainment. Whatever your Latte Factor is, you will need to figure it out and reduce or eliminate it for a time in order to get out of debt!

Protecting Your Assets

If you are a young professional just getting started or you have been in practice for several years, it is vital to lay a proper foundation to your financial life. There are two fundamental financial products used to implement a financial plan. These are investments and insurance.

Investments are the financial vehicles we use to build and accumulate wealth or to meet some other future financial goal such as college funding or retirement. Investment products are numerous and include things like stocks, bonds, mutual funds, real estate, precious metals and others. And of course, you can insure just about anything: cars, boats, houses, your income, your life. I even heard Mary Hart from Entertainment Tonight even insured her legs with Lloyds of London. Insurance products are purchased with the purpose of protecting your use and investment assets against loss.

Of course there are wills, trusts, business agreements, buy sell agreements, real-estate agreements, contracts, taxes, mortgages and many other things to consider in financial planning, but the two fundamental financial vehicles used to implement a financial plan are investments and insurance.

Take a look at Figure A on the next page. Imagine that your goal is to go from point A (where you are today) to point B (some period in the future – let's say, at a point of financial independence). The round ball you are looking at is your investment portfolio (or perhaps your net worth). Your job is to roll the ball uphill. As long as you roll the ball uphill it will grow larger and larger. This is good, because as the ball grows, your net worth increases and you get closer to reaching your goal of financial independence.

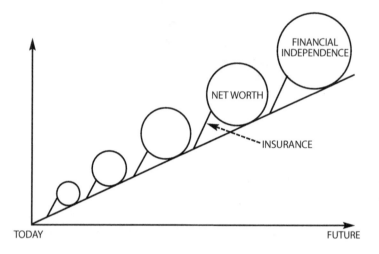

But let's say for some reason you are no longer able to roll the ball uphill, due to an illness or an accident. Well, without having someone who is capable of taking over for you, the ball is going to start to roll in the opposite direction (downhill). In this case however, the ball will begin to grow smaller and begin to break apart. Or perhaps you were to face some other catastrophic event such as a fire, a serious illness of a spouse or child, or any number of unfortunate events that could cause the ball to roll downhill and break apart.

One way to keep the ball from crashing to the bottom would be to install a braking system on the ball; the braking system in this case is insurance. If you have ever gone snow skiing you know that snow skis have a braking system to keep the ski from crashing down the hill should the ski come off when you fall. Insurance works the same way as a brake on a snow ski. Insurance catches the investment ball (your net worth) and keeps it from rolling to the bottom of the hill. The key is to be sure you have the braking system in place before you actually need it. Does this make sense?

It amazes me that people who would never think of driving a car without brakes, would even consider going without insurance to protect their lifestyle and their families as well.

Okay, so there are two fundamental financial products that are used to implement a financial plan, investments (which we use to grow our net worth) and insurance, which we use to protect our net worth. We will discuss investments in more detail in a little while, for now let's talk about some of the essential types of insurance that nearly every dentist should either carry now or at some time in the future.

Insurance

I know this probably isn't the most exciting topic we could be discussing, but in my opinion it is definitely one of the most important! At this point I am going to list several different types of insurance and then I will discuss each of them in more detail. My purpose is not to make you an expert in every area of insurance. However, I think it's important to provide you some basic knowledge about insurance products.

We are going to discuss:
- Life insurance
- Disability insurance
- Business overhead insurance (business disability insurance)
- Professional liability insurance
- Individually owned medical insurance
- Personal and business liability insurance
- Long-term care insurance
- Property and casualty insurance (auto, home, etc.)
- Umbrella coverage

Let's start with Life Insurance

Let me start by saying that if you don't have anyone who is financially dependent upon you, then your need for life insurance will be minimal. However for the purpose of this discussion I am going to assume that you have someone who is dependent upon you for his or her lifestyle now or that you will someday. There are two primary types of life insurance, term insurance and permanent insurance.

Term life insurance is generally issued for a specific term, thus the name. The most basic of term insurance is annually renewable term (ART). With ART the face amount, the benefit paid at death, stays level, for example at $500,000. But the premium increases annually as the insured gets older. Then there is what is commonly referred to as level term insurance (LTI). Like ART, the death benefit stays level, but with LTI the premium also stays level for a certain period of time. Most insurance companies today offer 5, 10, 15, 20 and 30-year level term insurance.

In my opinion a young dental professional would be wise to purchase 20 or 30-year level term insurance as they are getting started. It is very inexpensive compared to permanent types of coverage.

You can go to BridgingTheFinancialGap.com to see a spreadsheet showing the cost of $500,000 of 20-year level premium term life insurance for various ages of both men and women. By the way, if you smoke you should expect to pay 50-100% higher premiums, assuming you have no other health issues. Rates will vary from company to company and it is important that you know what is available to you. Your financial planner should be able to show you comparisons of the cost of policies from several highly rated insurance companies.

Here is an important point. In many cases some of the better known companies (i.e., New York Life, Northwestern Mutual, etc.) though they are excellent companies, tend to have term insurance that is more expensive than can be obtained by less well-known insurance companies. There are several excellent companies you may have never heard of that specialize in offering term life insurance. A few of them include Banner Life, First Colony Life, Transamerica Life and Genworth Financial. These are not the only companies that provide low cost term insurance, they are merely a few that I would suggest you have your agent look at for you. National associations (including the American Dental Association) also make this type of coverage available to their members.

When selecting an insurance company for life insurance try to use a company that is at least A+ rated from A.M. Best Company. A++ is the highest rating that an insurance company can earn from A.M. Best and I generally don't recommend using a company that is less than A rated. Your insurance agent should be able to tell you the rating of the insurance company he or she is recommending or you can find A.M. Best ratings on insurance companies at www.ambest.com. Of course you can simply call and ask the insurance company what their A.M. Best rating is.

There are many ways to purchase low cost term insurance. You can shop for insurance on the Internet, but I believe that using an independent insurance agent is the best alternative. In most cases you will not pay higher rates just because you are using an agent who is getting a commission to help you. Remember, not all insurance companies are the same and all insurance agents are not the same either, so be sure to find a good one. I recommend that you find an independent insurance agent that doesn't represent a particular insurance company, to help you find the best low cost coverage.

The second type of life insurance I mentioned is permanent life insurance. There are many different types of permanent life insurance. Here are a few:

- Whole life
- Variable whole life
- Universal life
- Variable universal life
- Current assumption whole life

In addition to providing a death benefit, permanent insurance builds what is commonly referred to as cash value. This type of life insurance has significantly higher premiums than term life insurance. One benefit of this type of coverage is the tax-deferred growth of the cash value and the favorable treatment for "loan based" withdrawals in later years of the policy.

The other major advantage of permanent life insurance is just that – it is designed to be permanent. That is, its purpose is to be in force when you die! This is really the main idea behind permanent life insurance. So, when purchasing permanent insurance you should buy it only if you intend to keep it in effect until you die.

Here's a very important point. Many dental professionals have been sold permanent life insurance policies for the purpose of using the cash value at some time in the future (i.e., for supplementing retirement income or for college funding). When they purchased these policies they were told about the great advantages of tax-deferred growth and "tax free" income through the use of policy loans. These are great advantages, however most insurance agents fail to disclose a very important fact. If the policy ever lapses or if you cancel it for any reason, the gains (cash value less premiums paid) will be taxed as ordinary income.

Now I'm not saying that you should not use the cash value in a permanent life insurance policy. I am only saying that you need to know what you are getting yourself into before you purchase such a product. When you are thinking about purchasing a permanent life insurance policy there are several factors that need to be considered.

1. What is your long-term need for life insurance? For instance, do you need to provide long-term security for a disabled child?
2. Will you need additional liquidity to pay estate taxes?
3. What can you reasonably afford to pay, both today and in the future?
4. What do you want from the insurance, other than the death benefit? For instance, are you looking for supplemental retirement income, or a source of loan funds?

In addition to the above factors there are other financial priorities that should be taken care of before purchasing permanent life insurance:
1. Your emergency reserve should be funded as I discussed earlier.
2. Other insurance coverage (discussed next) should be in place first.
3. You should be fully funding your retirement plan.

Be aware that there are many insurance agents and those that call themselves financial planners who sell life insurance to fund retirement plans. I am not in favor of this use of life insurance for several reasons, but to explain those here is beyond the scope of this book. At this point, just remember that insurance should be used to protect your assets and there are many more effective investment products that should be utilized to fund your retirement.

Individual Disability Insurance.

The next type of insurance that should be purchased is your individual disability insurance policy. In years past, there were several major disability insurance companies from whom you could purchase disability insurance, but today there are fewer. Here are two major policy provisions that you should look for in a quality individual disability policy:

1. **Non-Cancelable and Guaranteed Renewable** – with a non-cancelable policy the issuing insurance company can never cancel your policy (unless you don't pay the premium). In addition, the company can't increase your premium unless you increase your coverage. Most non-cancelable polices today offer level premium policies and step-rated polices. The step-rated policy will generally have a lower initial premium than the level premium policy, but then the rate will increase after a period of time, for example five years. Step-Rated policies can be good for young professionals,

but are generally limited to those individuals 35 years old or younger.

2. **True Own Occupation definition of disability** – a true "Own Occ" disability policy defines disability as the inability to perform the material duties of your occupation. This definition of disability will allow you to work in another occupation and continue to receive your disability benefits even if you are working in another occupation. Many policies offered today may reduce your benefit if you are earning an income in another occupation. These policies are commonly referred to as "Modified Own Occupation" policies.

Other policy provisions you should include in your personal disability policy are:

1. Automatic Increasing Benefit – This will help to keep your (pre-disability) monthly benefit up with inflation. Don't confuse this benefit with the Cost of Living Benefit discussed below.
2. Future Income Option – This rider will guarantee that you will be able (regardless of your health) to purchase more coverage in the future as your income increases.
3. Cost of Living Benefit – This benefit is designed to increase your disability benefits after you become disabled and should be a priority, especially if you have several years before you are planning to retire.
4. Lifetime Benefit Rider – (many companies no longer offer this benefit, but there are still some that do). If you cannot get a lifetime benefit you should have your benefits payable to at least age 65.

I generally recommend a 90-day waiting period on personal disability insurance policies also. A long-term disability is generally defined as a disability that last 90 days or longer. And this is what you are protecting against.

An important note – If you have a policy with a 90-day waiting period, don't expect the insurance company to send you a check on the 91st day of disability. Disability insurance companies pay benefits in arrears, which is at the end of the month. So if you have a 90-day waiting period, your benefits will start to accrue as of the 91st day; however, the insurance company won't issue you a check until the end of the 4th month of disability. This is one reason that you need to be sure you have an emergency fund.

When shopping for disability insurance, like life insurance, look at insurance companies that are rated A+ and A++ from A.M. Best. Some companies to include in your comparisons are Guardian Life, Berkshire Life, Mass Mutual, Principal Mutual and Unum/Provident. Again, this is not meant to be an all-inclusive list. Disability insurance companies change their underwriting policies frequently. The best company for disability insurance today may not be the best company tomorrow, so be sure to check the policy out before just picking a company. You can also check with various professional associations. However, you need to know that in most cases disability insurance provided by most associations are subject to change and are not true non-cancelable polices.

Question: *How much disability insurance should you buy?*

Answer: *As much as the insurance company will let you.*

There are three major reasons you should buy all you can. First of all, if you were to experience a reduction in income and then decide you want to purchase additional disability insurance, you may not qualify financially for an increase. The second reason is that most insurance companies will issue a maximum monthly benefit of $10,000, so it is important to get as much as you can, when you can. Third, if you were to develop a health problem it could preclude you from purchasing more coverage in the future. I have had several clients come to a point when they wanted more individual disability insurance coverage and they were unable to buy it for one of the above reasons. Therefore, I recommend you buy as much as you can, whenever you can.

As I mentioned earlier, most insurance companies will only allow you to purchase a monthly benefit of $10,000 and for many dental professionals a monthly benefit of $10,000 would be well below their existing income. One way to increase your coverage above the $10,000 limit is to purchase a group plan in addition to your individual policy. This type of coverage isn't available to everyone, but it could work for you. It is very important, however, that you must purchase the individual policy before you purchase the group coverage. Generally speaking, insurance companies will allow you to add group coverage on top of your individual coverage. However, when adding individual coverage on top of group disability insurance, insurance companies are more restrictive. It is essential that you work with an experienced disability insurance agent, as disability insurance can be very complicated and is not readily understood by most insurance agents.

The limits on coverage I have discussed do tend to change and some companies are now allowing for higher monthly benefits. A good independent insurance agent will be able to help you find the best coverage for your situation.

To deduct or not to deduct, that is the question.

I am often asked, "Are my disability insurance premiums deductible?" Yes, you can deduct your premiums, but only if your practice is established as a "C" Corporation. However, I do not recommend that you deduct your personal disability insurance premiums. If you deduct the premiums then the benefits are taxable when you receive them. But, if the premiums are not deducted then the benefits are received tax-free. The benefit that you get from the tax write-off is nowhere near the benefit of receiving tax-free benefits for the rest of your life. Therefore, I don't recommend deducting the premiums.

Another type of disability insurance that should be purchased early on in a dental professional's career is **Business Overhead Expense** insurance, often referred to as BOE. BOE is designed to pay office overhead expenses in the event the owner of the practice is disabled. Because it is designed to pay overhead expenses, BOE can only be purchased by a self-employed practitioner. An *employed* dental professional is not responsible for the overhead and therefore insurance companies will not even sell it to an employee.

I refer to BOE as "buy time insurance." Because what you are doing is buying enough time to determine what is going to happen to your practice while you are disabled. If you're only out for two or three months you will probably be able to recover somewhat quickly. But what if you're out of work for six, twelve or eighteen months? After all, you have employees who will want to continue to be paid, your rent or mortgage on the office has to be paid, and even your yellow page ad still needs to be paid.

BOE is less expensive than personal disability insurance. This is because you are not insuring these expenses for a long period of time, (i.e., to age 65) but usually only 12 to 24 months. You should analyze your overhead expenses closely and purchase a quality BOE policy. I recommend a 30-day waiting period and you should be sure to look at the same companies I mentioned earlier for personal disability insurance. This coverage is designed to pay overhead expenses and the premium is fully deductible.

Commonly covered overhead expenses include: rent, electricity, telephone, heat, water, laundry, salaries of employees who are not members of the insured profession, real estate taxes, interest on debt, depreciation or scheduled installment payments or principal of debt, installments, costs of furniture and equipment purchased or leased prior to the onset of the insured's disability.

Overhead expenses not covered include salary, fees, drawing account or other remuneration for the insured or any family member who was not a full-time employee continuously for the 60 days immediately prior to the insured's disability. Other non-covered items include the cost of goods (i.e., lab fees), or any merchandise, cost of implements or premiums that may be waived due to disability.

Another type of disability insurance that is relatively new is **Retirement Protection** coverage. This type of disability insurance is designed to fund a dentist's retirement plan in the event of a disability. Generally, insurance companies will allow you to insure your retirement contribution up to the maximum allowable contribution of a defined contribution plan. In 2006, this number is $44,000 per year (approximately $3,670 per month.) As the IRS increases the maximum contribution levels, insurance companies have generally allowed for higher protection amounts as well.

If you have already fully funded your retirement plan, there is no need for this type of coverage. But this would be well worth considering especially for someone who just started funding his or her retirement plan at a significant level. For a new dentist it's probably too early for this, but don't forget about it in the future.

You should also consider forming an alliance with a group of 3-4 other dentists in your area and agree (in writing) to cover for each other in the event one of you are sick or injured and can't work. A written agreement to cover for each other for 12 or 18 months could prove to be very valuable someday!

Individual Medical Insurance

It is my opinion that dentists should purchase an individual medical policy. Even if you are an employee, I strongly recommend you consider purchasing individual health insurance rather than being insured under a group plan. I learned this lesson early in my financial planning career.

My 48-year-old general dentist client, Jim, was insured through his office group plan with his wife listed as a dependent, along with three employees. Jim had a stroke and was never able to return to practicing dentistry. After determining he would not be able to return to work, Jim sold his dental practice for much less than its value was before he had the stroke. One day while discussing the medical benefits with the insurance company, Jim's wife, Nancy, casually mentioned that that they had sold the practice. Within a week they were notified that their health insurance was being cancelled. Why? Well because Jim no longer owned the practice and he was no longer "employed," his dental practice no longer met the definition of a "group." So Jim lost his group coverage. Fortunately the group policy had a clause that allowed him to convert his coverage to what is known as a conversion policy. However, he had to go from a $500 deductible and paying a premium of about $380 a month for himself and Nancy, to a $1,000 deductible plan that cost nearly $1,100 a month just for Jim alone. Nancy was able to purchase a less expensive individual medical plan. After two full years of disability, Jim qualified for Medicare and was then able to discontinue the expensive conversion policy.

Even with disability insurance this was a very difficult time for Jim and Nancy financially. I personally believe the risk associated with group insurance is too high for a self-employed individual.

Remember this about insurance companies; they are in business to make a profit. They can only operate profitably by bringing in more premiums or paying out less in claims. Pay the few extra bucks for individual coverage and protect yourself and your family from financial disaster! If you insist on a group policy, READ THE POLICY and know its limitations!

Incidentally, I complain about the high cost of my medical insurance like everyone else does. However, I had back surgery in February of 2003 and before all the write-downs from my PPO insurance plan, the total bills associated with my surgery and post surgery physical therapy were nearly $80,000, but my total out of pocket expenses were only about $1,500. Like I said, I don't like paying insurance premiums any more than anyone else. I do, however, like the benefits insurance companies provide.

Property & Casualty (Personal and Business)

When it comes to property & casualty insurance I have found that many dentists are underinsured and many are paying too much for the coverage they have. When purchasing property & casualty insurance there are several things you need to pay close attention to.

Be sure your coverage amounts are adequate. Here's one example of why. Let's say you have building contents worth $100,000, but you are only insured for $50,000. We'll assume your business policy has an 80% coinsurance clause for a partial loss (this is very common). We'll assume you have a $500 deductible and you suffer a $20,000 insured loss. In this situation the insurance company would pay the claim as follows:

$50,000 (loss) divided by $80,000 (80% of $100,000)
x $20,000 (loss) = $12,500
Less your $500 deductible leaves you with a check from the insurance company for $12,000. So in this case you suffered a $20,000 loss and only recover $12,000.

It is vital that you update your coverage regularly! This is a basic of good financial hygiene. So when your insurance agent sends you a letter that it's time for your annual checkup, don't ignore it. Just like you tell patients, prevention is the key, so pick up the phone and call your agent.

Be sure *everything* is covered. For instance many people think that items such as dirt bikes and quads are covered under their homeowners insurance. They're not! Be sure your property & casualty agent has an accurate list of your assets to assure that you are covered against loss of the asset, as well as any liability associated with owning the asset (i.e., dirt bikes, golf carts, etc.).

In regard to your business insurance, make sure you have business continuation coverage. For instance, if your building burns down, what will you do for income while it's being rebuilt? Business protection coverage could continue to pay your own salary as well as your key employees salaries for up to a year. Think of how those dentists in New

Orleans were affected by Hurricane Katrina. Of course they would have needed to have flood insurance, but this gives you an idea of what I am talking about.

Other things that you should be sure are covered are things such as employee dishonesty, employment practices liability and employee benefit liability coverage. These are just a few commonly overlooked areas to discuss with your property & casualty agent.

Here's another important point. If you double the amount of coverage you carry, your premiums don't automatically double as well. In fact, in many cases you can double or triple your policy limits for a few hundred dollars a year. Re-evaluate your coverage needs at least annually and be sure you have adequate or above adequate coverage.

Professional Liability Insurance

You should carry a minimum of $1,000,000 of professional liability insurance, and if possible, purchase an "occurrence" form policy. With this type of policy you may not have to purchase "tail" coverage like you would with a "claims made" policy (tail coverage can be expensive). If possible, you should purchase a policy that allows "defense" cost to be paid over and above your limit of liability. For instance, if you had a policy with a $1,000,000 and had a judgment against you for that amount, it would be beneficial to have your defense cost paid in addition to the judgment. In addition, extend your business umbrella coverage over your professional liability insurance if the carrier will allow you to.

Umbrella Coverage

An umbrella policy is designed to pick up where your other property and casualty insurance leaves off. You should have both a personal umbrella policy as well as business umbrella coverage. It is designed to protect you against a catastrophic event. This coverage is inexpensive and is a "no brainer" type of purchase for most dental professionals. Let's say you get into a car accident and accidentally kill someone. Well, $500,000 of liability coverage may or may not be enough and the opposing attorney may decide to go after your personal assets and/or future income. Umbrella coverage acts as an extra layer of coverage to protect your assets and future income. The higher your net worth, the greater your need for this type of very affordable insurance protection. However, younger dental professionals should not overlook umbrella coverage.

When it comes to property & casualty insurance, it's also worth noting that many insurance carriers give discounts when you have multiple policies with them.

Long-Term Care Insurance

Even if you are young, I'd like you to understand the importance of long-term insurance. Besides, you may someday be able to save someone else from the scenario I am about to describe, so please keep reading.

On March 9, 1996, I was sitting at my house with my mom and I was telling her that I would like to buy a long-term care policy for her. Her response was, "Larry, I'm not going to need that for a long time." At that time my mom had approximately $150,000 in invested assets, a condo valued at $75,000 and she was debt free. We discussed the matter briefly, but she was adamant that she wasn't going to need long-term care insurance for a very long time. I couldn't convince her to do it.

She went home that night thinking she wasn't going to need this insurance for a long time. Well she was right, if you consider twelve hours a long time. At 6:30 a.m. the next morning on March 10, 1996, I got a telephone call from my mom asking me to come over. She said she was having a difficult time breathing. My mom had asthma and she had experienced this before. So, I went over to her house, which was about a mile and a half down the road. When I got there, she was barely breathing. I got her into my car, and was literally driving 90 miles an hour on Greenway Road in Phoenix to get her to the hospital. It quickly became apparent that my mom was going to die. I pulled into a fire station, banged on the door and woke up the firemen. They came running out to my car. By the time they pulled her out of the car, she was dead. No vital signs, no signs of life at all! They placed her in the middle of the driveway of the fire station and started to work on her.

Although they managed to get her heart started again, they could not get oxygen into her lungs. Her lungs had collapsed and she ultimately went without oxygen for more than eleven minutes. Amazingly, she survived. Unfortunately though, she suffered anoxic brain damage and she became severely disabled. She was unable to walk, feed or dress herself. She wasn't able to even hold a spoon. She went from being totally financially and personally independent to being totally dependent on other people in every facet of her life.

After leaving the hospital, Mom was admitted to a rehabilitation facility to wean her off a ventilator. She was there for several months and received exceptional care. Eventually she was admitted to Christian Care, a long-term care facility in Phoenix, Ariz., where she lived for more than eight years until her death on December 21, 2004.

Before I go on with this story I want to make sure you understand something. I loved my mother dearly. In fact, she meant the world to me. Even as I write these words I cherish her memory and I don't want you to get the idea that my concern with this event was merely financial. I would have given all I had to keep her as I remember her.

Within 11 months of her asthma attack all of Mom's money was gone, approximately $150,000 and ultimately she qualified for Arizona's Medicaid plan for the indigent. At that time in Arizona, a single person was required to spend down their assets to less than $2,000 in order to qualify for what is called Arizona Long-Term Care benefits (ALTC). So once her assets (not including her home) were under $2,000, the state of Arizona paid her long-term care bill, which was approximately $3,500 per month.

A couple of years later, my mother's aunt died and left her a $250,000 inheritance. Approximately $140,000 of this would be spent on her care, until she again qualified for ALTC. (We were able to legally gift approximately $110,000 to other family members).

In short, approximately $290,000 of my mother's money was spent on her care until all of it was finally gone. A long-term care policy would have paid her more than $3,000 dollars per month, adjusted annually for inflation, for the 8½ years she was there! And yes, some of that $290,000 would have been used for her care, but a large portion of it (about $150,000) could have been used in many other ways, like helping to pay college expenses for her 21 grandchildren and four great grandchildren.

I share this story with you to give you an idea of what can happen to a person's life savings with an extended stay in a long-term care facility and to illustrate that the worst can happen (and it usually does) when we never expect it.

For married couples, it is even more important to plan appropriately in this area. If one spouse has to go into a care facility with costs running from $4,000 to $5,000 per month, the surviving spouse is going to be faced with a very uncertain financial future if they have to spend their retirement assets for long-term care expenses.

Now, if you don't have any assets to insure, there is no need for long-term care insurance. However, this type of coverage should definitely be considered for those who are already retired or within five to ten years of retirement and who have accumulated some significant assets. I suggest people start to investigate this type of insurance at around age 50. Premiums are relatively low at this age and for many people at this age, their children have begun to move out and are perhaps graduating from college, thus freeing up money to pay the premiums.

Like the other insurance coverage I have discussed, this type of insurance can vary greatly from company to company. Again, I recommend you work with an insurance agent who knows this type of insurance very well. And be sure to utilize a company that's rated very highly by the rating agencies.

Also, some insurance companies offer policies in which the premiums are paid for ten years and then are considered "paid up." This type of policy could work well for someone who is in their 50's or early 60's as they might be able to avoid paying premiums throughout all of their retirement years.

Here's something to consider. I have almost come to the point of ignoring "the averages." Day in and day out, I am not dealing with averages, I am dealing with individual people. I have two close friends who both had strokes before age 50. One was in a long-term care facility for nearly 6 years, until his recent death. His monthly care costs were nearly $4,000 per month and the only way his wife was able to keep most of the assets they did have was to divorce him. How sad!

Premiums for long-term care insurance can vary greatly from company to company. But, let's say you have a couple who are both age 65. They have a liquid net worth of $1,500,000. The husband has a severe stroke and goes into a long-term care facility. A 5-year stay will cost them over $273,750. That's @ $150/day for 5 years. A 10-year stay would be over

$500,000. That does not include medication, personal items, etc., and **it doesn't take inflation into consideration either!**

Let's say, however, that same couple purchased a long-term care policy at age 50 and paid premiums of $5,000/year ($2,500 each for ten years). Now they have a policy that will continue into their retirement years and they have the peace of mind that their life savings won't be eroded away by long-term care costs. If they spent $50,000 in premiums over a ten-year period they would come out way ahead if just one of them were to go into a care facility for even one year. I look at long-term care insurance as "disability insurance" for your retirement years. Don't overlook this important asset protection insurance!

This section on insurance is not intended to be all-inclusive. My goal is to encourage you to check out your insurance needs and insurance coverages carefully. An annual update of all your insurance coverage's is just as important to your financial well being as seeing your dentist at least twice a year is to your dental health.

Retirement Planning

I don't think there is any doubt that you know if you want to enjoy retirement some day, you are going to have to save some money. So I'm not going to go into this long dissertation on why you need to save money for retirement. There's an old saying, "If it is to be, it's up to me." And the fact is, in relation to retirement planning, this statement has never been truer.

So when and how do you get started? First of all, the sooner you get started the better. Why? The magic of compounding interest, that's why!

One of the best examples I can give you of someone who started early and will be rewarded greatly during her retirement is my sister, Jeri. Jeri isn't a dentist but she has accumulated a great deal of money over the last 27 years. And the amazing thing is she's done it on less than half the income of most dentists I know.

I recently visited my sister in Des Moines, Iowa. (By the way, I don't recommend going there in February if you can avoid it.) When I got to Jeri's home she met me at the front door, saying to me, "I'm a half-a-millionaire!" I looked at her and said, "what?" "I'm a half-a-millionaire," she said again, as she showed me her 401(k) statement. Her statement showed she had $502,000 in her account. "Wow, I said, you are half a millionaire! Way to go Jer!"

How did she accumulate $502,000? She did it with the magic of compound interest. My sister started saving one percent of her income at age 22 when she was making about $1.70 per hour and as her income increased she gradually increased her savings rate. Now at age 49, she is saving about $8,000 per year and has over $500,000 in her retirement plan. And here's another amazing thing. It took her 27 years to accumulate $500,000 during a period when the Standard and Poors (S&P) 500 averaged approximately 11.5%. In the next 10 years, if she averages only a 7.2% return and without saving another dime, her account will grow to over $1,000,000! And if she averages 11.5%, it will grow to nearly $1,500,000. That is truly amazing!

So with this example, it might be enough to say, as one of my favorite actors Sean Connery said in the movie, *The Untouchables,* "Thus endeth the lesson!" Start early and don't stop saving.

How Much Money Do I Need to Save?

Okay, you know you need to save money and you know you need to start early. So where do you go from here? First of all, it is important for you to know what type of retirement plans and investment vehicles are available to you. You will notice I referred to retirement plans and investments. Let me first point out that these two words are not interchangeable. I will start by briefly explaining the difference between the two. I know this is elementary for some of you, but think about how you felt when you did your first root canal, everyone has to start somewhere, so hang in there for a minute.

I'll use a car as an illustration to explain the difference between retirement plans and investments. With any car you will have a chassis and an engine. Everything within the car is wrapped around the chassis. The chassis in retirement planning is the plan itself, for example, the IRA, SEP-IRA, Profit Sharing Plan, 401(k) plan, etc. The plan tells you what you can and can't do. It tells you how much you can invest in to receive a tax deduction. It tells you whether or not you have to contribute money for your employees as well as other things. In essence, it tells you what the rules are.

The "engine" in retirement planning is the investment mix of the portfolio of your retirement plan. An investment portfolio may be made up of stocks, bonds, mutual funds, certificates of deposit, real estate, etc. All of these investments help run the plan and determine its performance. So what is the fuel? The fuel is CASH! Cash is what you use to purchase the investments to fund your retirement plan.

One question that you may be asking at this point is, "How much money do I actually have to save (invest) in order to reach my retirement goal?"

Well, the answer to this question will be different for everyone and how much you will need to save depends on several factors:

1. At what age do you wish to retire? (How much time do you have before you wish to retire?)
2. What amount of income will you need (or want) at retirement?
3. What other income sources will you have at retirement? (i.e., Social Security, rental income)
4. What rate of return do you expect to earn on your investments before retirement?
5. What rate of return do you expect to earn on your investments during your retirement?
6. What assets have you already accumulated for retirement?
7. What is the projected tax rate of your retirement assets when they are liquidated?
8. What is the projected rate of inflation?

As you can see there are several factors to take into consideration when attempting to answer the question, "How much money do I actually need to save in order to reach my retirement goal?" Once you have the answers to the above questions then there are several calculations to be conducted in order to determine how much savings will be required. The calculation of how much money you will actually need to save in order to meet your retirement objective is critical to your planning process. However the methodology of this calculation is well beyond the scope of this book. My purpose here is to give you some key items to think about. It is my recommendation that you seek the help of a qualified financial planner to help you with this calculation.

Note: Not all retirement expenses are affected by inflation in the same manner. For instance, if you have the same house and a fixed mortgage payment when you retire, then your house payment will not be adversely affected by inflation. Actually it will be just the opposite. But a great number of other expenses, such as medical insurance, auto expenses, groceries, and utilities will definitely increase in cost over time.

Before attempting to determine how much money you will actually need to retire, you will first need to determine how much income you want (monthly or annually) at retirement. I will be totally honest with you though, determining this amount is not an exact science and this amount is dependent on several different factors, many of which are nearly impossible to forecast. For instance, who knows what Social Security will be like 10, 20 or 30 years from now. Who knows what tax rates will be or what health care will cost? The best you can do is to make some assumptions based upon your current expenses and how you expect them to change in the future.

Retirement planning is an ongoing process. You will need to continue to update your situation on a regular basis. My best recommendation to you is to find a competent planner who you enjoy working with and meet with them at least once a year to update your plan. By the way, I don't think it's a necessity to live in the same state as your advisor. With technology today it is very easy to have a distance relationship with your financial planner. So, if you have one who you like, you shouldn't change just because you move or they move.

Below are some questions to ask yourself when determining your desired retirement income:
1. What are my current expenses? (Refer to your expense summary worksheet)
2. What expenses will be eliminated by the time I retire? Hopefully, the expenses of children will be gone. Perhaps your home will be paid off by then.
3. What will be some new expenses that you will have? For instance, will you take more vacations?
4. What expenses will increase? Will health care costs be higher?
5. What are some personal expenses currently being paid for through my practice (i.e., auto expenses, health insurance, travel expenses, other)? There are probably several personal expenses that you currently pay for through your practice. I encourage you to put together a list of these items. I think you'll find it's more than you think.
6. What should I expect from Social Security? Obviously if you are a thirty-year-old dentist your Social Security benefit probably isn't as secure as if you are a sixty-two-year-old dentist.
7. What tax deductions will you lose? Think about it, the three largest tax deductions that you will have during your working lifetime are your business deductions through your dental practice, your children and your home interest deduction. Once you retire you will lose business deductions. Hopefully, your children will be on their own by then, though this is not always

the case. And if you haven't paid off your mortgage by the time you retire it is likely that your interest deduction will have decreased significantly by the time you retire.

There are several other things to keep in mind regarding retirement. For instance, a great number of my retired clients find they have more time on their hands and start up new hobbies or revisit old ones. Many have become more involved in their communities. In addition, some of their activities at retirement cost less than many of the activities they participated in when they were working. For instance, many tend to eat at home more than they did when they were working. After all, eating at home is less expensive and we tend to enjoy cooking more because we are not in such a hurry to get somewhere. In addition, with the increased time available, people are better able to plan vacations and they learn to travel less expensively. Think about it, when you have time to shop for vacations you do a better job at it than when you are trying to manage your practice, your family and other things all at the same time.

Something else that I have experienced time and time again with newly retired clients is that they become more conscious of the money they are spending in general. I believe this is due to some sort of psychological instinct to spend less when you're not working to create income. After all, you've been working your whole life and now where is the money going to come from? Over time though, they become accustomed to living off their net worth and adjust very well to their newfound freedom. I'm sure you will too!

"Qualified" vs. "Non-Qualified" Investing
You may have heard the terms "qualified" and "non-qualified" in regard to investments. Let me briefly explain the difference between these two terms. For the purpose of our discussion, qualified investments are those investments that are held in some sort of retirement plan, such as an IRA, SEP IRA, Simple IRA, 401(k), or Profit Sharing Plan. Qualified investments generally allow the investor to receive a "qualified" tax deduction against their income when the investment is made, and in addition, qualified investments grow tax deferred. I will discuss various qualified investments in much more detail shortly.

Non-Qualified Investments
Non-qualified investments, simply defined, are those investments that

are not being held in a "qualified" retirement plan. They are those investments purchased outside of a qualified plan with after-tax dollars. There are many reasons you will want non-qualified investments in addition to qualified investments.

The first reason is liquidity. Non-qualified investments typically are not subject to early withdrawal penalties from the IRS (an exception is the growth on non-qualified annuities.) So, if you need to use money from your non-qualified investments before age 59½ it is usually readily available. Of course, the tax treatment of non-qualified is different than qualified investments. Generally speaking, non-qualified investments are taxed as they grow. The growth will be taxed as either ordinary income or as capital gains, depending on whether the growth is coming from dividends or capital appreciation, or whether you have a short-term or long-term capital gain. Typically, short-term gains are taxed as ordinary income and long-term gains are taxed at capital gain rates, which are usually lower than ordinary income tax rates. There are also certain investments that may provide tax-free income, such as municipal bonds and mutual bond funds. At this point we won't go into further detail on the tax treatment of non-qualified investments.

Qualified Retirement Plans
Now let's discuss some of the most common "qualified" retirement plans. Before I go into detail on the various types of retirement plans, there are some common characteristics to all of these that you should know. First of all, with the exception of the Roth IRA, all of the plans discussed here can be funded with pre-tax dollars. That is, the contributions are tax-deductible, and the money that goes into them as well as the growth is not taxed until it is withdrawn at retirement.

Another important thing you need to remember is that when you put money into a qualified retirement plan or an IRA, the plan does not come with an ATM card! This money is meant to stay there for retirement. As such, withdrawals made prior to age 59½ years old are subject to ordinary income tax plus an additional excise tax of 10% (25% in Simple IRA's for pre-mature withdrawals made in the first 2 years). Therefore, if you are in a 35% marginal tax bracket and you withdrawal $10,000 from your plan prior to age 59½, you would be required to pay ordinary income taxes of $3,500 plus an additional $1,000 in excise taxes for a total of $4,500, netting you only $5,500 on a $10,000 withdrawal!* You may also be subject to state income taxes as well.

Before attempting to pick the plan that is best for you, there is a very basic question you need to ask yourself. How much money do you realistically plan to save? If you are just getting started, it probably isn't realistic that you will be saving $40,000 per year in a profit sharing plan. That would be nice, but more than likely there are other priorities like paying off debt and accumulating an emergency reserve, that are more pressing right now. However, if you have been in practice for some time and have paid down your debt then you may be able to commit to saving a larger percentage of your income. The key is to determine what is a realistic contribution that you can commit to. Early in your career, you may start by funding an IRA and as your income increases, you may move to a plan that allows for substantially higher contributions, like a profit sharing plan or even a defined benefit plan.

Okay, let's talk about some of the most popular retirement plans available to you.

Individual Retirement Accounts (IRAs)

Let's start with the individual retirement account, commonly referred to as an IRA. If you are only going to be saving $4,000 per year or less, then a traditional or Roth IRA will work just fine for you. The maximum contribution in these plans for 2006 is $4,000 if you are under age 50 and $5,000 if you are 50 or older. Be sure to check with your CPA to verify your eligibility for these plans.

Both of these IRA's are easy to set up and they are generally very cost effective. However, the tax treatment of these two IRA's is very different.

The Traditional IRA

The traditional IRA is most often used as a tax deductible IRA for someone with earned income or by a spouse of someone with earned

---

* Section 72T of the Internal Revenue Code allows a person to take distributions (under certain circumstances) from a retirement plan before the age of 59 1/2 without the 10% excise tax on distributions that is normally imposed on distributions taken prior to age 59 1/2. I advise that you seek the advice of your CPA to determine under what circumstances you would be eligible to take early distributions and avoid the early withdrawal penalty.

income, as long as they are not participants in a qualified retirement plan. The traditional IRA grows tax-deferred. That is, you won't pay income tax on the growth until you take money out of the account in the form of a distribution.

If you are eligible and under age 70½, you can take a current tax deduction for all or part of your contribution. A full deduction is available if you aren't covered by an employer-sponsored retirement plan. If you're covered by a plan, you can still take a deduction against your taxes if your modified adjusted gross income (MAGI)* is less than a certain amount. The IRS changes this amount on a regular basis, so you will want to check with your tax professional to determine whether or not you are eligible for a deductible IRA. (In 2006 the amount is $50,000 if you're single and less than $75,000 if you're married and filing jointly.)

Also, if you're married and filing jointly and either you or your spouse is covered by a retirement plan, the spouse who isn't covered can make a fully deductible contribution in 2006 as long as your combined MAGI doesn't exceed $150,000. The deduction is phased out at $160,000. These figures are adjusted regularly by the Internal Revenue Service, so be sure to check with your CPA as to what amount, if any, you can contribute to a tax deductible IRA.

Roth IRA
Contributions to Roth IRA's are not tax deductible. That is, you save with after-tax dollars. However, when you withdraw your money, generally it won't be taxed. The idea is to pay taxes upfront, but never have to pay taxes on the growth. You can contribute the full amount ($4,000 in 2006, $5,000 if you are age 50 or older) to a Roth IRA as long as your MAGI doesn't exceed these limits:
- $95,000 if you're single
- $150,000 if you are married and filing a joint return

The contribution is fully phased out at $110,00 if you're single and $160,000 if you're married and filing a joint return.

---

*To arrive at your MAGI, start with your adjusted gross income (AGI) on your tax return and talk with your tax advisor to find out how the AGI gets changed (or modified) by certain losses or deductions.

So which IRA do you choose? If you're eligible for both a traditional IRA with deductible contributions and a Roth IRA, consider using a Roth IRA if you:

- Don't need the immediate savings of a tax deduction
- Think you will be in the same or higher tax bracket in retirement.

There are many things to consider when deciding whether to fund a Traditional or Roth IRA. Generally, if you are in a 15% marginal tax bracket or below, I recommend the Roth IRA. Remember, the maximum contribution amounts are adjusted annually by the I.R.S., so be sure to consult your financial advisor or CPA when deciding which is best for your situation.

Simple IRA'S

If you are able to save more than the traditional and Roth IRA limits, then a Simple IRA plan may work for you. A Simple IRA will allow you to save 100% of your income up to $10,000 per year (in 2006) as an employee, even if you're self-employed. And if you are 50 or older there is also a "catch up" provision that will allow you to defer an additional $2,500 of income per year. Again, these numbers are subject to change so be sure to check with your CPA to determine the annual maximum contributions that you are eligible for.

In addition to an employee deferral, the Simple IRA also has a required employer contribution. The employer has the option of selecting one of two options available under the Simple IRA rules, but they must choose one of these.

The first option is to make a contribution that is equal to 2% of income for all employees, regardless of whether they are participating (making employee deferrals) in the plan or not. The other option is for the employer to make dollar for dollar matching contributions of up to 3% of salary for only those employees who are making salary deferrals in the plan. Personally I have found that the 3% matching option is used most commonly.

Let's take a look at how a Simple IRA Plan might work for a typical dental office. Here's the makeup of the office:

	YEARS WORKED	ANNUAL INCOME
Dr. Jones (Age 51)	4 Years	$150,000 (Salary)
Becky – Hygienist	4 Years	$50,000
Tammy – Receptionist	6 Months	$15,000
Debbie – Dental Assistant	3 Years	$26,000
Rhonda – Dental Assistant	2 Years	$22,000

We will assume that there is a 2-year waiting period in order to be eligible to participate in the Simple IRA Plan and that Dr. Jones chose to make a 3% matching contribution. Let's also assume that all eligible employees (everyone but Tammy) are maximizing their contributions. Dr. Jones would be eligible to make a contribution of $12,500 as an employee ($10,000 plus a catch-up contribution of $2,500) for his own account. In addition, he would make his employer contribution to his own account of $4,500 (3% of his $150,000 salary) for a total contribution of $17,000 to his account. In this case Dr. Jones would also be required to make a total contribution for his employees of $2,940.

Dr. Jones' contributions to his employees' accounts are limited to a matching contribution to a maximum of 3% of salary for those employees who are participating. In this example, we assumed all eligible employees are maximizing contributions so his contribution is $2,940 (3% of $98,000). The $98,000 figure was determined by adding the eligible employees' annual incomes together, $50,000 + $26,000 + $22,000. Remember, in this case, Tammy would not be eligible, because she has only been employed for six months and not for the 2-year waiting period.

It is also important to note that only actual "salary" is included when determining the employer contribution. So, for instance, if you are a Sub S Corporation and you have a salary of $80,000 and distributions of $70,000 for a total income of $150,000, only the $80,000 salary can be used when determining your employer contribution.

For 2006, the maximum salary that can be used to determine employer contribution is $220,000. Another important thing to remember is that the employer contributions to a Simple IRA are immediately "vested" to the employee. So, if the employee quits or is fired, the employer contribution to the plan goes with them in their account.

SEP IRAs

I rarely recommend SEP IRA's and the reason is simple. With the SEP IRA, whatever you save for yourself (i.e., a percentage of your income), you are legally required to do the same for any employees who have worked for you for three out of the last five years. In addition, money you save for your employees is also immediately "vested" just like the Simple IRA. The SEP IRA usually requires the employer to make much higher contributions to employee accounts than other plans. This combined with the immediate vesting often make the SEP IRA unattractive to many dentists. The maximum contribution in 2006 for a SEP IRA is the lesser of $44,000 or 25% of your gross pay. (Remember, shareholder distributions are NOT considered salary and therefore cannot be included when determining your gross pay.) Although I don't see them being used as much as in the past, a SEP IRA does work well in some cases; so don't rule it out until you check out its possibilities first.

401(K) Plans

The 401(k) plan is probably the most well known of all retirement plans. A 401(k) plan allows employees to contribute a portion of their compensation on a pre-tax basis. Like the other plans already discussed, salary deferrals are not subject to federal income tax when contributed and, in most states, are not subject to state taxes. In addition, the interest and appreciation earned on the contributions grow tax-deferred until the participant withdraws the money from their account. In 2006, an employee (including the dentist) can contribute up to $15,000 to a 401(k) plan ($20,000 if age 50 or older).

It's rare that I recommend a 401(k) plan by itself for dental offices. The reason is, 401(k) plans can significantly limit the amount of salary deferrals of highly compensated employees (of which the dentist will most likely be) if there is not enough participation from other employees. Therefore, 401(k) plans by themselves are generally more appropriate for very large dental practices. However, when combined with a profit sharing plan (discussed below) a 401(k) plan can work very well.

Profit Sharing Plans

A profit sharing plan is a retirement plan in which the employer (the dentist/owner) makes contributions for the benefit of him or herself and their eligible employees. Even though it is called a "profit-sharing" plan, you are not required to actually have a "profit" in order to make contributions to the plan.

Profit sharing plans have several benefits. First of all, the employer contributions to the plan are discretionary. That means that a fixed contribution is not required every year. In fact, in lean years you can even skip contributions when your income may be down significantly.

The profit sharing plan may include a variety of creative designs on how contributions are allocated to employees, including the ability to benefit different classifications of employees at different contribution levels so long as certain discrimination tests are passed. Terms like 'integrated' plan, 'cross-tested' plan, and 'new comparability' plan, all refer to unique allocation formulas for profit sharing programs.

I believe one of the best benefits of the profit sharing plan is that it allows the owner to contribute a substantial amount of tax-deductible dollars on an annual basis into the plan for him or herself. In 2006, the maximum contribution to a profit sharing plan is $44,000. In addition to the employer contribution, a profit sharing plan can include a 401(k) option as discussed above; however, with a 401(k) option the maximum contribution remains at $44,000 (in 2006). When coupled with a 401(k) option though, the dentist can make an "employee" contribution of up to $15,000 (in 2006), therefore reducing the "employer" contribution by the same amount. The benefit to the dentist is that it will reduce the doctor's contribution required to the employee accounts as well. This will allow him or her to maximize their personal contribution and help to reduce the contribution made to the employee accounts by the dentist.

Another benefit of a profit sharing plan is that it allows the employer to utilize a vesting schedule. Vesting is an employee's right to the ownership of the contributions that the employer made to the plan on the employee's behalf. There can be immediate vesting, where the employee has immediate ownership. In other words, if the employee leaves the employer (voluntarily or not) than the employer's contributions go with the employee.

The other type of vesting is delayed vesting. With delayed vesting, the employee must stay with the employer for a certain number of years before they are fully "vested" in the employer's contribution. There are two basic types of delayed vesting schedules. There is cliff vesting, where the employee has no ownership rights until a specific period of time has elapsed (i.e., 3-year cliff vesting). Then the employee becomes 100% vested in the employer's contributions. The other type of delayed vesting is graded vesting where the employee becomes vested over time. Here's a typical graded vesting schedule:

YEAR OF SERVICE	% VESTED
1	0%
2	20%
3	40%
4	80%
5	100%

Of course employees are always 100% vesting in their own contributions to any retirement plan.

As I mentioned earlier, the amount that you are going to be able to actually fund on an ongoing basis should be a major factor when deciding what type of retirement plan you should consider.

So how do you pick the best plan? The first thing you need to do is to prepare a census of your practice. This census will include a list of all your employees (including yourself), their date of birth, date of hire, hours worked per year, and annual income. Below is a sample census form. If you would like a blank form to use for your office, simply go to BridgingTheFinancialGap.com and go to "FORMS."

Dr. _____

Employee Name	Birth Date	Hire Date	Hours Worked	Annual Compensation

Okay, now that you have your census completed, what's next? At this point you have two options.

Option One

If you are a "do-it-yourselfer," then you will need to hire a Pension Administrator to determine how different retirement plans could work in your situation. I recommend that you use a pension administrator in your area. To find a pension administrator you can go to www.aspa.org, which is the website for the American Society of Pension Administrators, or www.nipa.org, which is the website for the National Institute of Pension Administrators. Note: A pension administrator is not a financial planner. The pension administrator's job is not to develop a comprehensive financial plan or to manage your investments. They are analyzing your census data and providing scenarios of how various retirement plans might work for your situation. Once the retirement plan is installed, the pension administrator manages the plan. In other words, the pension administrator makes sure you are following the rules according to the IRS and Department of Labor. This also includes preparing tax returns (Form 5500) for the plan itself on an annual basis.

Option Two

Option two is to give your financial planner your census and have him or her work with the pension administrator. Let them do the work for you! Another benefit of having your financial planner do this for you is that they should already have the entire picture of your financial situation and they should be well equipped to identify what plan is most appropriate for your situation.

Asset Allocation/Investment Selection

Okay, so you know you are going to have to save some money in order to achieve the various financial goals you have for yourself and your family. So how do you go about choosing the investments to fund your goals? I mentioned early on in this book that there are many different types of investments: stocks, bonds, mutual funds, real estate, as well as others. I also mentioned early on that this book is not designed to help you pick the best stocks. However, I do think it's important that I at least get you on the right track.

For many people, choosing the right investments can be very confusing. Many people think that the objective of investing is maximizing return and minimizing the risk. Well, this is only partially correct. The object of investing should be to obtain a desired result. That is, you should design your investment portfolio to achieve a desired result. Let's say, for instance, that you want to begin saving for your 3 year old daughter's college education. You have determined that you will need to save $80,000 by the time your daughter reaches age 18. So you have 15 years to accumulate $80,000. In this example, we'll assume that you can save $250 per month toward this goal and your required rate of return would be 7.1%.

Therefore, instead of just trying to maximize your return, you should develop your investment portfolio to earn within a certain targeted range, like 6% to 8%, or 10% to 12%.

Know Your Goal
Here's a real life example of why this is important. My clients, Andrew and Karen, had accumulated a significant investment portfolio by the time I met them. They were trying to figure out whether or not they could afford to retire. After completing their retirement analysis I deter-

mined that they needed to earn 6% on their investments in order to accomplish all of their retirement goals. At the time, the vast majority of their investments were in growth-oriented mutual funds. Why? Because that is what their broker told them would provide the greatest long-term return. Well, that's NOT what they needed! Six percent is what they needed.

Incidentally, I met Andrew and Karen in 1998, two years before the start of one of the worst bear markets in the history of the U.S. stock market (April 2000 – September 2002)! Just trying to maximize long-term returns is not what investing is all about!

My point is that your portfolio needs to be designed to achieve a desired result, not just maximize return and minimize risk. Before I go any further with this discussion, I need to make something very clear; developing an investment portfolio takes time. The other day, I saw a television commercial from a large discount brokerage house and I was shocked to hear their spokesman say that at "their firm," they can help you develop an investment portfolio in the time "it takes to make a cup of coffee." Their point was they could do it fast and they could do it cheaper than Charles Schwab, Merrill Lynch or anyone else for that matter. As John Stossel of 20/20 would say, "Give me a break!"

Investment Risks - Control What You Can

If you think about it, one of the biggest concerns to an investor would be not reaching their investment objective in their time horizon (i.e., accumulating enough money to retire at age 60). Investing nearly always entails some level of risk. There are three basic portfolio risks that can prevent you from reaching your investment objectives; they are:

1. Capital risk (i.e., the possibility of losing principal).
2. Inflation risk (i.e., the chance of lost purchasing power resulting from negative inflation-adjusted returns).
3. Reinvestment rate risk (i.e., the risk of reinvesting income and principal at low rates of return).

How much exposure to each of these risks is right for you? This question is complicated because of the inherent trade offs between these risks. For instance, if you choose to invest in U.S. treasury bills in order to reduce capital risk, you will increase your exposure to reinvestment rate risk and possibly to inflation risk as well. The key is to be sure that you (along with your advisor if you use one) prioritize the importance of protecting against each risk and base a statement of investment objectives on those objectives.

Here's something to think about. When investing, there are things that you can control and there are things you cannot control. For instance, you can control how much money you save, but you cannot control the fluctuation of the stock market. You can control your investment allocation, but you cannot control the price of gas. There are many uncontrollable factors that reduce the possibility of reaching an investment objective and eroding your investment portfolio. However, I believe that when managing your investments the key is to focus on what you can control rather than on what you can't. When I was about 8 years old, my older brother David told me something that I will never forget. He said, "Larry, most of the things that happen in life are beyond your control. Your job is to control what you can and learn to live with the rest."

One approach in developing the right investment mix is utilizing asset allocation. The premise behind asset allocation is pretty simple. Don't put all your eggs in one basket. Think about this, why are there nine defensive players on a baseball field? Why not just a pitcher and catcher? Answer: Because no one knows where the ball is going to be hit, that's why! Having nine players on the field also increases the chances of the team being successful, which is keeping the other team from scoring in this case. Just like there is no sure way of knowing where the baseball is going to be hit, there is NO WAY of telling what asset classes are going to perform the best in any given year.

Implementing an investment strategy, utilizing asset allocation, is generally done through a process of assessing your investment time horizon and risk tolerance through a series of questions relating to each. When the asset allocation is complete, a range of probable returns can then be determined. Once this is done, you can then determine whether your goal(s) can be achieved within this range of returns. If so, then it may be appropriate to proceed with implementation of the asset allocation model. If not, you then must either; adjust the goal, (i.e., retire later or live on less income) or be willing to accept more risk in the allocation in order to potentially achieve a higher rate of return.

The process of asset allocation is intended to help you identify what percentage of your portfolio should be invested in each broad asset class. It is my opinion that this process is best completed with the assistance of a qualified investment professional. However, there are also several good books on the market that can be of help to those of you who wish to do it yourselves.

Following are five Morningstar® "broad" asset allocation models. These are only samples and are not meant to be recommendations. They are merely shown here as an illustration of how asset allocation models can vary.

Very Aggressive

Asset Class	Allocation %
• Cash	0
• U.S. Stocks	80
• Non-U.S. Stocks	20
• Bonds	0
• Other	0
Total	100

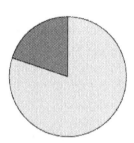

Aggressive

Asset Class	Allocation %
• Cash	0
• U.S. Stocks	68
• Non-U.S. Stocks	17
• Bonds	15
• Other	0
Total	100

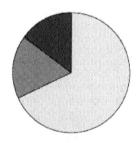

Moderate

Asset Class	Allocation %
• Cash	0
• U.S. Stocks	52
• Non-U.S. Stocks	13
• Bonds	35
• Other	0
Total	100

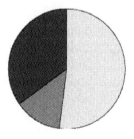

Conservative

Asset Class	Allocation %
• Cash	15
• U.S. Stocks	40
• Non-U.S. Stocks	10
• Bonds	35
• Other	0
Total	100

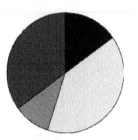

Very Conservative

Asset Class	Allocation %
• Cash	20
• US Stocks	24
• Non-U.S. Stocks	6
• Bonds	50
• Other	0
Total	100

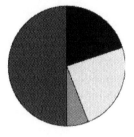

Below is a list of commonly used (specific) asset classes in modern portfolio theory.

Stocks/Stock Mutual Funds
Large growth
Large value
Mid cap growth
Mid cap value
Small cap growth
Small cap value
Real estate
International stocks
Emerging markets

Bonds/Bond Funds
Short-term bonds
Intermediate bonds
Long-term bonds
High yield bonds
International bonds

Cash
Regular saving accounts
Money market instruments
Certificates of deposit

No one can always predict precisely which asset class will be the strongest or weakest of the year. By diversifying across asset classes, you put yourself in a better position to benefit from the best-performing asset class and it will also help to reduce the overall volatility of your portfolio.

The Case for Diversification

Year	U.S. Stocks	Global Stocks	Bonds	Asset Blend*
1984	+6.3%	+5.8%	+15.1% B	+9.1%
1985	+31.7	+41.8 B	+22.1	+31.9
1986	+18.7	+42.8 B	+15.3	+25.6
1987	+5.3	+16.8 B	+2.8	+8.3
1988	+16.6	+24.0 B	+7.9	+16.1
1989	+31.6 B	+17.2	+14.5	+21.1
1990	-3.1	-16.5	+9.0 B	-3.6
1991	+30.4 B	+19.0	+16.0	+21.8
1992	+7.6 B	-4.7	+7.4	+3.5
1993	+10.1	+23.1 B	+9.7	+14.3
1994	+1.3	+5.6 B	-2.9	+1.3
1995	+37.5 B	+21.3	+18.5	+25.8
1996	+22.9 B	+14.0	+3.6	+13.5
1997	+33.4 B	+16.2	+9.7	+19.7
1998	+28.6 B	+24.8	+8.7	+20.7
1999	21.0	+25.3 B	-0.8	+15.2
2000	-9.1	-12.9	+11.6 B	-3.5
2001	-11.9	-16.5	+8.4 B	-6.7
2002	-22.1	-19.5	+10.3 B	-10.5
2003	+28.7	+33.8 B	+4.1	+22.2

Sources — U.S. Stocks: the S&P 500; global stocks: MSCI World Index; bonds: Lehman Brothers Aggregate Bond Index. *An equally weighted blend of the S&P 500, MSCI World and Lehman Brothers Aggregate Bond indexes.

The table above illustrates the case for investment diversification.
As the table shows U.S. stocks outperformed global stocks and bonds for seven of 20 years with four years of negative returns. Global stocks outperformed U.S. stocks and bonds for eight out of 20 years with four

years of negative returns. Bonds outperformed U.S. stocks and global stocks for five out of 20 years with two years of negative returns.

If you had a blended portfolio with 1/3 in U.S. Stocks (S&P 500)*, ⅓ in Global Stocks (MSGI World Index)* and ⅓ in bonds (Lehman Brothers Aggregate Bond Index)*, the return of the blended portfolio would have been higher than the lowest performing of the three indices in each and every year from 1984–2003. *Remember however, past performance is no indication of future results!*

By the way, I am not recommending that you allocate your investments as discussed above. Instead, I highly recommend you seek the advice of a qualified investment professional when designing an asset allocation model.

The need for asset allocation doesn't end once you have accumulated enough money to retire. The truth is, it can be even more critical due to the fact that when you retire, you now become dependent upon your assets to provide you with income. For instance, Manning & Napier, a registered investment advisory firm in Rochester, NY, compared the effect (and risk) of taking fixed annual withdrawals of $80,000 from two different portfolios. Each portfolio started with $1,000,000. The first portfolio is 100% stocks and the second portfolio a 50% Stock and 50% bond blended portfolio. (See chart on next page.)

The time period they used was from 12/31/1972 – 12/31/2003. (A 30-year time frame). Although the stock portfolio had a higher average annualized return of 11.2% during the time period, it was actually depleted by the end of 1995. That is, by 1995 the account had a zero balance. The blended portfolio however, had a lower average rate of return (10.3%) during the same period; and it never ran out of money. In fact, it had an ending balance in excess of $1,000,000 at the end of 2003.

So, with the 100% stock portfolio, had you taken a fixed amount of $80,000 from your portfolio, you would have run out of money in 1995. However, if you had a portfolio of 50% stocks and 50% bonds and taken a fixed amount of $80,000 per year at the end of 2003, you would have still had a portfolio worth over $1,000,000. As I said earlier, asset allocation is vital to portfolio management, especially during the distribution phase of retirement planning.

The Risk of Fixed $ Withdrawals $80,000 Annual Withdrawals

Year	Market Value 100% Stock Portfolio (11.20% Avg. Return)	Market Value 50% Stock/50% Bond Portfolio (10.30% Avg. Return)
1972	$1,000,000	$1,000,000
1973	$781,165	$869,667
1974	$506,320	$700,395
1975	$603,850	$771,171
1976	$659,866	$825,693
1977	$534,457	$722,250
1978	$486,116	$677,289
1979	$488,380	$668,795
1980	$546,382	$696,850
1981	$441,156	$628,837
1982	$435,184	$690,311
1983	$446,284	$708,055
1984	$388,577	$692,027
1985	$417,011	$781,029
1986	$408,876	$828,316
1987	$359,898	$799,529
1988	$333,645	$806,186
1989	$344,848	$895,343
1990	$253,996	$842,963
1991	$238,177	$945,588
1992	$170,122	$931,279
1993	$102,576	$946,173
1994	$21,616	$847,353
1995	$0	$982,659
1996	$0	$1,015,782
1997	$0	$1,134,003
1998	$0	$1,273,114
1999	$0	$1,308,867
2000	$0	$1,247,720
2001	$0	$1,146,894
2002	$0	$1,011,925
2003	$0	$1,077,174

Complete depletion of assets with 100% in stocks. Analysis performed by Manning & Napier. Source S&P 500 and 50% S&P 50 and 50% Intermediate Government Bonds data provided by Ibbotson.

Once you have selected the appropriate asset allocation, you then need to pick what you believe to be the best investment alternatives within each asset class. The actual investment products that are available as "non-qualified" investments are generally the same as "qualified" investment alternatives. Some of the most common investment vehicles are: stocks, bonds, mutual funds, and annuities. There are literally thousands of investment alternatives that fall under one or more of these investment vehicles and all of them have their place. As stated early on in this book, it is not my purpose here to teach you how to pick the best investment vehicle(s). It is, however, very important to be sure you do one of the following before you begin investing in any of the alternatives I mentioned:

1. Educate yourself. There are myriads of investment books available and countless websites, magazines, and other sources to go to if you want to "do it yourself."

2. Hire an investment professional to help you. I favor this option, however, this is not an easy undertaking. My best recommendation to you in this area, is to talk to several colleagues or other people you know that have had success finding a qualified investment professional, and interview several of them before selecting someone. By the way, just because someone holds a particular license or works for a particular firm does not necessarily make him or her a "qualified" investment professional. I will discuss in more detail what to look for when looking for a financial advisor a little later.

After you have developed an appropriate asset allocation and selected the appropriate investments within each asset class, it is important that you review your asset allocation on a regular basis (perhaps quarterly, semi-annually or annually). The reason is, as your investments in your various asset classes move up and down in value, your asset allocation will change and over time these changes can become significant.

For instance, let's say you have four asset classes represented in your portfolio. To make things simple in this example, we will assume you have your portfolio divided equally (25% in each) among four broad asset classes at the beginning of the year: Large cap stocks, small cap stocks, international stocks and bonds. See the chart on the next page.

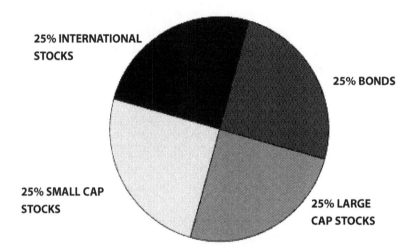

For the sake of this example, let's say that your bond and your international stock holdings remained unchanged by the end of the year. However let's assume that your large cap stocks increased in value and your small cap stocks decreased in value, thus causing your portfolio allocation to change. By the end of the year let's say that your portfolio looks like the chart below:

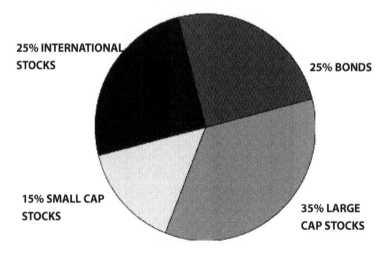

If your investment objective hasn't changed, then your portfolio may now be "over exposed" to large cap stocks and "under exposed" to small cap stocks. In order to bring your portfolio back to the original allocation, you will need to sell off some of your large cap stocks and (buy) small cap stocks. This process is commonly referred to as "portfolio re-balancing." It's important to understand that portfolio re-balancing will not necessarily increase your rate of return. The main purpose of portfolio re-balancing is to maintain the asset allocation that has been determined to be most appropriate for your situation.

Paying for Investment Advice

There are basically two types of investors: The first are those who want to design their own portfolios by some process of investment selection that they have either read about, attended seminars on, or designed themselves. Then there are those investors who are going to hire someone to implement an investment process for them. These next few paragraphs are for those who would prefer to hire someone to help them.

First off, let me say this. I believe that if you are going to hire someone to help you, then you should expect to pay him or her for that help.

If you want investment advice and haven't really accumulated much in assets, then you should expect to pay some sort of commission. It's hard for financial advisors to charge a fee on a small investment account. For instance, if an advisor charged 1% per year on a $20,000 investment account and prorated the fee quarterly, it would be hard to stay in business – the annual fee would be $200. If the account were billed on a quarterly basis, then the quarterly fee would be about $50. This type of arrangement would make it nearly impossible for an advisor to stay in business.

A point here about "loaded" mutual funds: If you are working with a commission-based investment advisor and using mutual funds, I generally recommend that you use what are referred to as "A" share funds. With "A" share funds you will pay a front-end charge; however, the internal expenses of an "A" share will be less than it's comparable "B" or "C" share. In addition, as your investment account increases (within a mutual fund family), the front-end sales charge will decrease as you hit what are referred to as break points. With "B" and "C" shares, although there is no upfront expense, they do have higher internal expenses, which will lower your rate of return over time. It is my opinion that in most cases, you will be much better off using "A" shares for long-term investing.

Another way to pay for investment advice is under an asset based fee arrangement. If you have a portfolio of $100,000 or more, this may be an option for you. With an asset based fee arrangement, rather than paying commissions, you pay your advisor an agreed upon fee, which is generally a percentage of the assets they are managing for you. With this type of fee arrangement your investment advisor buys and sells mutual funds without commissions charged to the investor. For situations like this, many traditional, "loaded" mutual fund companies have special arrangements in which they waive the up-front sales charge or offer special share classes for this type of arrangement. Therefore, you as the investor, could buy a traditional "A" share at net asset value (that is without the upfront sales charge). Of course, the investment advisor may also buy and sell traditional "no-load" mutual funds or individual securities like stocks and bonds for you under a fee arrangement as well.

In most cases, the advisory fee charged is based upon the size of the investment account being managed, with larger accounts being charged less (as a percentage of assets) than smaller accounts. A graded management fee is typical, but there are some advisors who charge a flat fee regardless of the amount invested (i.e., a flat 1%). Below is an example of a graded fee schedule.

Fee Schedule

Up to		$350,000	1.35%
$350,000	to	$500,000	1.20%
$500,000	to	$750,000	1.00%
$750,000	to	$1,500,000	0.90%
$1,500,000	to	$2,500,000	0.75%
$2,500,000	and above		0.60%

Here's something to consider; buying investments can be somewhat like buying a car. If you have $10,000 to buy a car, then your choices are going to be limited to cars priced at or below $10,000. If you have $100,000 to buy a car with, then you have a lot more choices. The investment world can be very similar. Those who have more money, generally have more investment options available to them. Regardless of where you are today, you need to know what your options are. Don't be afraid to ask your advisor exactly how they get paid. After all, your patients ask you don't they?

What's My Practice Worth?

This is a question I am asked a lot. I'll be honest with you though, this is not my area of expertise. However, this could very well be one of your largest assets. And, like any other asset, you should have your practice evaluated regularly (about every five years). This can be very helpful for several reasons, including estate planning and for the eventual sale of the practice itself. For the purpose of this discussion, when I refer to your practice in this section, I am referring to your patient base and the tangible assets. I am not including the actual building and land where the practice is located. I will say though, if you can, I highly recommend you work to own your own building as well as the real estate. This will very likely increase the value of your practice; as well as provide possible tax benefits and a future stream of retirement income.

The process of placing a value on a dental practice can be somewhat complicated. There are three common methods to value a dental practice. It is typical of most valuation experts to use some combination of all three when valuing a practice. The three valuation methods are the income approach, the excess earnings approach and the market approach. As I said, I am not an expert in this area and the process for using these valuation methods are beyond the scope of this book. There are many companies and consultants across the country that specialize in valuing and selling dental practices. My recommendation to you would be to find three or four of them who specialize in your area and interview them before just picking someone to help you. I think it is very important to also interview some of their past clients as well. When selling a dental practice, you don't want to just arbitrarily pick someone to help you and I don't believe you should "go it alone." The difference to you could be thousands of dollars!

So what do you do to increase the value of your practice? First of all, you should begin planning your exit as soon as you make your entrance into your new practice. What I mean by this is that you need to build your practice in such a way that someone will want to buy it. This means establishing good practice management techniques from the get go. This starts by paying close attention to the details of your practice. For instance, there are certain statistics that you should track regularly, either weekly or monthly. This includes statistics relating to patient flow, expenses, overhead ratio, the number of new patients per month, and your account receivables ratio. Certain expenses in your practice are directly related to, and will fluctuate with, your revenues. These include dental supplies, lab fees and staff salaries. Once again, a good practice consultant will help you with these guidelines.

Now tracking these statistics in and of themselves is meaningless if you don't actually do something with them. You should look for trends in these statistics (i.e., are your profits growing as your expenses are increasing?). Do more employees equate to more profit? Is your hygiene revenue at least 25% of your total revenues? Over time, these statistics should show you whether you are on a growth pattern or not. For instance, in the first 10 years of practice you should be seeing at least 5% growth per year in profitability.

Be aware that 75% – 80% of the value of your practice can be based on "good will," so you need to be sure you have plenty of it! If you are within 10 years of retirement, here a few things you should be evaluating to be sure your good will has maximum value:
1. Where's your practice located? Is it in a desirable area? Do you see any indications that the area could be declining? Should you consider moving the practice to a more desirable area? Can you recoup the expense of a move?
2. How's the appearance of the office? Is it clean? Is the furniture, flooring, etc., in need of repair or replacement? Could the office use a face-lift?
3. Is the staff happy? Do they get along with each other? Are they a cohesive team?
4. Is it time to bring on an associate? Will he or she work well with your existing staff? Are you both on the same page for where you want to take your practice?

If you are at the point of bringing on an associate, you should highly consider someone who is new, right out of dental school. This should be an individual that your patients can come to know and trust over time, just like they have come to know and trust you over time.

Before hiring an associate (who you hope to sell the practice to later), I also recommend that you have your practice evaluated so that when it comes time to turn over the reigns of the practice, you will have a very good idea of how much growth the new associate was actually responsible for. This will be key when working to establish a price to sell the practice to the associate down the road.

Make sure you keep accurate financial records and try not to "mingle" too many personal expenses onto the practice expense books. Personal expenses that are commonly included as business expenses by dental professionals include: personal life & health insurance, auto expenses, interest expense, and legal expenses. If other personal expenses are run through your practice, be sure to document these expenses well. Specific documentation of all personal expenses will allow an appraiser of your practice to deduct these, thus increasing your bottom line and ultimately the value of your practice.

Another good idea when bringing on an associate who is planning on buying the practice someday, is to hold back a portion of their income (maybe 5%) to use as a future down payment on the practice. Obviously the new associate would have to agree to the idea, but it could be a good way to help them save some money as well as give you an indication of how serious they are about buying the practice down the road.

Once the practice is sold to the associate, it is common for the "selling" dentist to become the "associate" dentist and work on a limited basis to help in transitioning the practice to the new "owner." This helps the new dentist to maintain patients and gives the "exiting" dentist some time to transition their life as well.

Here are two more suggestions. First, don't "carry back" a portion of the loan. There are too many things that can happen that are beyond your control when you are no longer the owner of the practice. And if you don't want the chance of having to take back the practice, then eliminate that chance by having the buyer secure his or her own financing. Secondly, I highly recommend you make sure you have some sort of hobby before you leave your work. I have witnessed on many occasions, dental professionals who retired and then re-entered the profession because they were bored.

College Funding

For those of you that have kids and want to plan for their college expenses, there are two tax-favored college funding plans I recommend you investigate. The Coverdell Education Saving Accounts (formerly Education IRAs) and the 529 Savings Plan. The one that's most appropriate for you depends on several things. For instance, how much you want to invest and how often you want to move your assets among funds. Before choosing one, I recommend you speak with your financial advisor before deciding. Below are brief summaries of each plan:

529 Savings Plan
- Earnings and withdrawals for qualified higher education expenses are free from federal tax.[1]
- There are no income limits. You can contribute no matter how much you earn.
- Up to $11,000 ($22,000 for married couples) can be contributed each year without gift-tax consequences, and under a special election, up to $55,000 ($110,000 for a married couple) can be contributed at one time by accelerating five years' worth of investments.
- You maintain control of the assets. You decide when the money will be spent.

Coverdell Education Accounts
- Earnings and qualified withdrawals for education are free from federal tax.[1]
- You can invest $2,000 per year.
- You can use assets to pay school expenses from private kindergarten through high school,[1] as well as college and graduate school.
- There's flexibility to change investment options as often as you wish.

Most experts agree that Coverdell Education Accounts and 529 savings plans are excellent college savings vehicles. My biggest caution to you is to be sure you don't over fund your children's' college fund and under fund your retirement plan!

---

1 These tax benefits are effective through 2010 unless extended by congress.

Taxes

They say that the only two things that are certain in life are death and taxes. Taxes are one of those things that affect nearly everyone, we all pay them, but the truth is few people really understand them.

Tax planning is, of course, a major part of any comprehensive financial plan. The purpose of this section is not to show you all of the ways to reduce your tax bill. Instead, I want to help you understand two important concepts relating to income taxes.

The first concept is quite simple. You will pay income taxes and you will pay a lot of income taxes over your lifetime. You will pay income taxes on your earned income as well as on various unearned income sources, (i.e., capital gains tax, interest income and other investment related income). So get used to it. The point I want to make here is this: Don't let the "tax tail" wag the "investment dog." During my years in the investment world I have experienced more than one occasion where a person was reluctant to sell an investment because they would have to pay income taxes on the gain. This is allowing the "tax tail" to wag the "investment dog."

One of the best examples I can give you is during a time when we were experiencing a raging bull stock market. Tech stocks had soared in value and many investors just didn't think it would stop. I remember talking with an engineer at Intel. He was about 45 years old. He had a significant amount of his 401(k) plan invested in Intel stock (approximately $500,000) and he owned an additional $1,000,000 in Intel stock in vested stock options. He had visions of early retirement, travel, and life on easy street.

I recommended that he diversify a large portion of his Intel stock, both in his 401(k) plan and with his vested stock options. However, he didn't want to do it. Why didn't he want to sell his Intel stock? Two reasons. First of all, he didn't see how Intel could possibly go down. Secondly, if he exercised his stock options (outside of his 401(k) plan) and sold the Intel stock, he would have to pay approximately $100,000 in income taxes. Instead, he held the stock and watched as Intel went from a high of approximately $75 per share to under $20 per share about 2 years later. So, instead of selling the stock and paying taxes, his $1,000,000 in stock options dropped by 75 percent. This story has two lessons; one, what goes up, will come down. And two, don't let the "tax tail" wag the "investment dog!"

The Marginal Income Tax

I believe the most important tax concept you should be aware of is the marginal income tax. When asked how much they pay in income taxes most people will respond with a percentage rate of some sort, 30%, 40%, or 50%. What they are usually referring to is their marginal income tax rate. Simply defined, the marginal income tax rate is the rate at which the next dollar you earn will be taxed. This is very different than your average tax rate, which will always be lower than your marginal tax rate.

The chart below illustrates the 2005 federal marginal income tax rates. It's important to understand that when referring to the marginal income tax rates, we are talking about the tax rates that are being applied to your taxable income. Your taxable income is the income that you actually pay income taxes on. Your taxable, income in simple terms, is your income after business deductions, and after allowable exemptions and allowable itemized deductions. Your taxable income will always be less than your gross personal income. You can generally find your taxable income on page two of your federal tax return.

Federal Marginal Tax Rates for 2005

	Single	Married - Filing Joint	Head of Household	Married - Filing Separate
10%	0–$7,300	0–$14,600	0–$10,450	0–$7,300
15%	$7,300–29,700	$14,600–59,400	$10,450–$39,800	$7,300–$29,700
25%	$29,700–$71,950	$59,400–$119,950	$39,800–$102,800	$29,700–$59,975
28%	$71,950–$150,150	$119,950–$182,800	$102,800–166,450	$59,975–$91,400
33%	$150,150–326,450	$182,800–$326,450	$166,450–$326,450	$91,400–$163,225
35%	$326,450+	$326,450+	$326,450+	$163,225+

The U.S. income tax system is a graduated tax system. That is, as your taxable income increases your tax rate increases as well. Although I have provided you the tax rate brackets for 2005, you can also go to BridgingTheFinancialGap.com to get an updated Marginal Income Tax Rate Chart. The above chart illustrates that not all of your income is taxed at the same rate. For instance, for a husband and wife filing a joint tax return with a taxable income of $135,000 in 2005 their income tax would be calculated as follows:

0 – $14,600	is taxed at 10%	=	$ 1,460
$14,600 – $59,400	is taxed at 15%	=	$ 6,810
$59,400 – $119,950	is taxed at 25%	=	$ 15,138
$119,950 – $135,000	is taxed at 28%	=	$ 4,214
Total Tax equals			$ 27,622

So what is the benefit of knowing your marginal income tax rate? Knowing your marginal income tax rate can be helpful in several ways. First of all, it will allow you to determine the after-tax cost of a business expense. For instance, let's say you are in the 28% federal tax bracket and your state tax rate is 4%; combined your marginal tax rate is 32% (28% + 4% = 32%). Let's assume that you are anticipating purchasing a new office computer system that has a price of $20,000. The calculation below shows you that your after-tax (savings) cost will be $13,600 with a combined (federal and state) marginal tax rate of 32%.

Cost of computer system*	$ 20,000	
Less tax savings	$ 6,400	($20,000 x .32)
After tax cost	$ 13,600	

*Sales tax not shown

The same calculation will also provide you the after-tax cost of making a contribution to a qualified retirement plan such as an IRA, Simple IRA or Profit Sharing Plan. Let's say you were going to make a contribution to a Profit Sharing Plan for yourself. (We'll say for now that you are the only eligible employee.) If you were going to make a contribution of $40,000 and you are in a combined federal and state marginal tax bracket of 32%, then a $40,000 contribution into your plan will only require an after tax savings contribution of $27,200.

Profit sharing contribution	$ 40,000	
Less tax savings	$ 12,800	($40,000 x .32)
After-tax cost of contribution	$ 27,200	

For a $4,000 IRA contribution the numbers would look like this:

IRA contribution	$4,000
Less tax savings	$1,280
After-tax cost of contribution	$2,720

Knowing your marginal tax rate is very helpful for year-end tax planning in that it can help you determine whether you should pay expenses in the current year or hold off paying expenses until the following year. For instance, if you have had a great year, you may want to pay expenses in the current year to enjoy higher tax savings. Or conversely, if your income in the current year has been unusually low, then you may want to defer paying some expenses until the next year when you expect that your taxable income will be higher.

Another benefit of knowing your marginal income tax bracket is that it will help you to determine whether or not you should defer income in a particular year. For example, suppose it's December of 2005, you are retired and you currently have an estimated taxable income of $58,000. You have decided that you would like to take a two-week vacation to Hawaii in January 2006, which will cost you $10,000. In order to pay for the trip, however, you will have to withdrawal additional funds from your IRA account. Let's assume you are married filing a joint return.

Referring back to the marginal tax rate chart, you can see that if you were to withdraw more than $1,400 from your IRA in 2005, this will cause you to move from the 15% marginal tax bracket up to the 25% marginal tax bracket. Depending on your projected income for 2006, it may be better for you to pay for the trip in January of 2006 rather than December of 2005.

Of course, there are many other tax issues that you will be faced with at some time in the future; however, at this point, it's not my intention to make you a tax expert. Also, remember the tax laws change on nearly an annual basis so it is imperative that you seek the advice of a qualified tax advisor to help you in this area.

Estate Planning

Of all the things I discuss in this book, this is definitely one of the most important. In fact, with nearly every financial plan I write, this is the area that I address first and foremost.

Every adult, especially if they are married, should have a will. And it is extremely important that you have a will if you have children. There are four estate-planning documents that nearly every adult person should have. And I believe a qualified estate-planning professional should prepare them. These are not documents that should be self-prepared, purchased online, from a stationery store, or prepared by a document preparation service company. The four documents are:
1. Will
2. Living will
3. Medical power of attorney
4. General (financial) power of attorney

Let's talk about each of these separately.

Will

One of the main things that I want to point out regarding a will is that if you don't have one drafted for yourself, most states will draft one for you. Most states have what are referred to as intestate statutes. These statutes apply when a person has failed to do any planning. Basically, they say that if you die without a will the state will decide how your estate will be distributed. In addition, if you have children, they will also decide who will be the guardian of your children and the conservator of the assets you have left for them. By the way, the guardian and the conservator can be different people.

The purpose of a will is pretty simple. Your will states who gets what, when you die. In addition, your will allows you to designate the person who will be the guardian of your children as well the person who will manage the money, (including life insurance proceeds if your children are the beneficiaries) and the terms of distribution. It is very important to be sure your will (and all other estate-planning documents) are kept current.

Living Will

The main purpose of a living will is to provide medical providers with your desires as they relate to certain life saving and/or life sustaining measures in the event you are unable to make those decisions for yourself (i.e., if you were to become incapacitated). The underlying idea behind this instrument is that it allows you to make these decisions while you are in the right frame of mind as opposed to leaving these decisions up to a spouse, children or other family members while they may be in an extreme emotional state. As with the other documents we are discussing in this section, the living will is really for the benefit of your family and helps make very difficult decisions easier.

Medical Power of Attorney

Simply put, a medical power of attorney allows someone else to make medical decisions for you when you are unable. These decisions are not necessarily related just to life saving measures, but could also include things such as what particular course of medical treatment should be taken. It is very common for medical powers of attorney and living wills to be completed when someone is in an emergency room being admitted to a hospital. I have a close personal friend of mine who is a surgeon and on more than one occasion, he has had to ask a family member of the patient whether or not he could proceed with removing a limb of a patient or to perform certain surgical procedures. Believe me, this sort of thing happens hundreds of times every day! A medical power of attorney can't fully replace your personal decision process in regard to your wishes, but at least with the medical power of attorney, there is someone you trust making the decisions for you.

General (Financial) Power of Attorney

In most cases, a general (financial) power of attorney only takes affect when someone becomes incapacitated and usually has to be accompanied by letters from at least two physicians stating that the person is medically or mentally unable to handle his or her affairs. You really need to be sure you select the right person to act as your agent under your general power of attorney. You need to be sure that you trust them emphatically. For instance, if I named my sister Jeri as my agent under my general power of attorney, then Jeri would have the full authority to do with my assets whatever she wants. Of course, Jeri is legally required to act on my behalf and for my benefit. Although improper, if she wanted to spend my money and go on vacation she could very easily do that, even though she might not be acting appropriately. Of course, the intention is to select a person that you believe would make decisions that are in your best interest and that those decisions would be reasonably close to what you would do.

Let's look back at my mom's situation. On March 10, 1996, my mother's life changed dramatically as a result of an asthma attack that left her without oxygen for more than 11 minutes. From that moment on, she was no longer capable of making her own decisions personally in relation to her medical care, her assets or her personal finances. Two days after her asthma attack that left her with irreversible brain damage, my five sisters, my older brother and I were all together for the first time in 24 years. After about three days together with the emotions that we were faced with and with our mother still in coma, the questions naturally began to surface. Questions like, "What are we going to do? What are we going to do about Mom's house? What about Mom's assets? Will she have to go into a care facility? How are we going to pay for everything? What about this? What about that?"

Here's what happened. I went in to my filing cabinet and said, "Here's what we're going to do." And I began to read my mothers estate-planning documents (she had previously executed her will, living will, medical power attorney, and a general power of attorney) starting with her general power of attorney. My mom had raised seven very independent children and she had planned for an event of this very sort. As I read the documents, it was very clear this wasn't me speaking, this was mom. There was no confusion, no unanswered questions, and no arguments. Mom was very clear how things were to be handled and by whom. The point I want to make here is that my mom didn't have these documents prepared just for her, but for us seven children as well. She did it for us. By having her affairs in order, even while she was in a coma, she was able to continue to keep peace at home and not leave her children wandering, "What do we do now?" Mom had left clear directions, and though it wasn't necessarily easy for us in every regard, it definitely made things a lot easier.

I mentioned earlier that I do not believe that you should buy these estate documents at some office supply store, or use a software program to prepare them. I highly recommend that you use a qualified estate-planning attorney who is very familiar with the laws of your state. There are many reasons, and I have personally witnessed how self-prepared estate-planning documents have caused more problems, and have ended up costing people more money than they could have ever saved by not using a qualified attorney. Let me give you a real life example.

Recently, I had a lady come to my office. She was not a client of mine, but she knew me. Her ex-husband was admitted to a long-term care facility at the age of 55 due to a severe stroke. Prior to their divorce, she was named as the beneficiary on his IRA account and life insurance, as well as the agent under his general power of attorney. After the divorce, it was his desire to keep her as his beneficiary as well as the agent under his general power of attorney. But guess what? They had used a software program they had purchased to prepare their estate-planning documents and there were several problems that came up as a result. First of all, even though the documents were correct, he did not have his signature witnessed. The software company did not tell them that the state of Arizona requires that these documents be witnessed in addition to being notarized. So, even though the documents were notarized, his signature was never witnessed; therefore, in Arizona the documents were considered null and void.

In addition to that, his life insurance and IRA's beneficiary designations were also made when they were married. Remember, this was her ex-husband. The estate planning laws in Arizona state that if you are married and your spouse is the beneficiary of your life insurance or any other asset that is passed by a beneficiary designation, or payable upon death, (i.e. IRA', annuities, retirement plans, as well as many other assets) if you subsequently get divorced, you must sign a post-divorce beneficiary designation if you wish to have your ex-spouse remain as your beneficiary. If you don't, then the original designation no longer applies. In this case, he had $250,000 in his IRA account and a $100,000 life insurance policy. But, due to the fact that the beneficiary designations were not reconfirmed after their divorce, she was now (legally) no longer the beneficiary on his IRA account or his life insurance.

Fortunately for her, I referred her to a qualified estate-planning attorney who was able to assist her in getting the appropriate documents executed. She was also very fortunate that her ex-husband was still mentally competent and therefore capable of executing the documents. Three weeks after completing the appropriate paperwork to keep her as the beneficiary of his accounts, he died. Had the correct documents not been executed, it is very possible that his assets would have been left to someone other than whom he wanted them to go to.

My point in relating this story to you is simple. Don't put yourself (and your family) at risk by attempting to prepare your estate planning documents yourself or trying to complete your estate planning without the direct involvement of a qualified estate-planning attorney. This is not the place to save a few dollars. The amount of money you'll save in legal fees is not worth it! In fact, it could end up costing you much more later. In addition, you need to know without a doubt that your estate-planning documents are going to work the way you want them to when you really need them to!

OTHER TRUSTS

In addition to the documents already discussed, there are two other documents that are commonly used in estate planning. They are the revocable and irrevocable trusts. (Note these documents do not replace any of the documents we have already discussed, but may be used in addition to them.)

Let's discuss these briefly.

Revocable Trust

Below are some important benefits of using a revocable trust:

1. First of all, assets placed in a revocable trust escape probate. That is, a revocable trust allows you to transfer the use and /or ownership of your assets to another person immediately upon your death without any court proceedings. This is done by naming a successor trustee within the trust document. Note: a "will" does not accomplish this by itself.

2. A revocable trust is a private document. A will, on the other hand, is a public record once it has been filed. That means that anyone who wants to can get a copy of your will. They can't do this with a trust.

3. A properly structured revocable trust may also help to reduce or possibly eliminate estate taxes.
4. A revocable trust avoids conservatorship proceedings and the cost and time associated with those proceedings.
5. A revocable trust allows you to decide when and how your beneficiaries will receive distributions from your estate. In contrast with a will, when a child reaches the age of majority (typically age 18), the conservator must distribute the remaining assets to the child. This may or not be what you want!

It is important to note that you do not have to give up any rights to any property that you place within a revocable trust. Generally speaking, when you create a trust, you will be the beneficiary and the trustee of the trust while you are living. Furthermore, it is important to note that just having a trust does not accomplish anything. After the trust is executed, you must then go through the process of what is commonly referred to as "funding the trust." This process simply requires that you transfer title of the assets you want in the trust from your name (i.e., John Doe) to the name of the trust (i.e., The John Doe Revocable Trust, dated January 5, 2005). Most estate planning attorneys will help you or show you how to get this accomplished.

Irrevocable Trust
The main purpose of an irrevocable trust is to reduce estate taxes. It is very important to know that once you place an asset in an irrevocable trust you cannot maintain any incidence of ownership. That means you cannot have any direct access to the asset including any say as to how the asset is to be used. In fact, you are giving up total control of the asset to the trustee of the irrevocable trust.

It is very common to have life insurance policies owned by an irrevocable trust; this allows the death benefit of a life insurance policy to be free from estate taxes in addition to being free from income taxes. Note: Life insurance is, in most cases, free from income taxes even without the use of any type of trust. Though life insurance is the most common asset placed in an irrevocable trust, other assets can be transferred or purchased by an irrevocable trust as well.

Due to the fact that estate tax avoidance is the main purpose of an irrevocable trust, it is very important to consult with a qualified estate planning or tax attorney before any such trust is even considered.

Your Trusted Advisory Team
or Your Financial Quarterback

What is your number one asset? When I ask this question, many dental professionals respond with answers like, "my home," "my practice," or "my employees." Wrong! You are your number one asset. You are the most valuable asset you have! And your next most valuable asset(s) are your professional advisors. Your advisors help you make your smartest financial decisions both personally and professionally. They help you make your practice more profitable. Your advisors will help you make your practice marketable should you decide to sell it. They'll help you build your practice into a business that is not based solely on you and your ability to generate income.

Your *Trusted Advisory Team* is made up of several different professional members:
- Attorney
- CPA
- Insurance agent(s)
- Investment advisor
- Practice management advisor
- Financial planner

All of these people play an important role on your trusted advisor team. However, the objectives of each team member are very different from one another. For instance, your attorney will to want to make sure that you have the appropriate legal documents in place to protect you personally and professionally. In addition, your attorney will want to be sure you have the appropriate estate planning documents so that your desires will be met in the event of your disability or death.

Your CPA's goal will be to make sure that you file your tax returns on time and in such a fashion as to allow you to pay as little in taxes as you legally have to. Your insurance agent will want to be sure you are adequately protected against various types of risks, while minimizing your insurance premiums. Your investment advisor will try to provide the best return on your money within your risk tolerance levels. And your practice management advisor will be working to improve the overall productivity of your dental practice with the ultimate goal of increasing your revenue and your profits. And finally, the role of the financial planner is to bring all of these team members together to function in such a way to accomplish these objectives in a coordinated effort to give you the highest probability of achieving your financial goals.

Your Financial Planner Is Your Quarterback

In most team sports, there is usually one person (a position player) who calls the plays. In football, this person is usually the quarterback. The quarterback, of course, is taking direction from the team coach. However, even though the quarterback is involved in every play, he doesn't actually run the ball every play himself. Instead, the quarterback takes direction from the team coach; he then brings the team together in a huddle in order to let everyone on the team know what play is being called, who is going to get the ball and when. The quarterback then executes the play along with the rest of the team, thus allowing the team to effectively move the ball up the field in a coordinated effort.

Your financial planner acts as the quarterback of your advisory team. You provide direction to the financial planner—your values, your goals, and your dreams. The financial planner executes your financial game plan in a coordinated effort with the rest of the advisory team, with the objective of moving you over your goal line. This makes sense, doesn't it?

Here's another illustration of the value of a financial planner. I live about 13 miles from my office and there are several different routes I can take in the morning to get there. So, in order to determine the best route on a given day, and in order to avoid traffic delays, I will usually listen to the traffic report before even leaving my house. Why? Very simple–I want to avoid problem areas where there may be an accident, road construction or some other problem causing a traffic jam.

The reason I am able to avoid these delays is because from the sky, the helicopter traffic reporter can see the big picture of my route to work. The role of the financial planner is very similar. The financial planner is the person on your advisory team who will have the big picture of your entire financial life. He or she will also be able to see the most favorable route to reaching your goals as well as see possible financial road hazards ahead of you and help you avoid them, thereby increasing your chances of actually achieving your desired results.

In essence, a financial planner works very much like a general dentist. The general dentist designs and oversees a treatment plan; the financial planner designs and oversees the financial plan. There will be certain procedures that the general dentist will perform, such as extractions, crowns, or on-lay build-ups. But there will be other procedures, perhaps endodontic treatment, orthodontics or periodontal treatment that might be referred to a specialist. The financial planner will implement certain elements of the financial plan, maybe retirement plan design or investment management. But in many cases they will refer you to a specialist like an estate-planning attorney for estate planning documents, or a CPA for certain tax related issues. With dental care there is one person, the general dentist, who oversees the overall care of the patient. The general dentist designs and then coordinates the treatment plan in a systematic fashion in order to gain the best result for the long-term care of his or her patient. And the financial planner designs and then coordinates the financial plan in a systematic fashion in order to gain the best result for the long-term financial health of his or her client.

With a dentist or a financial planner it is, however, up to the patient or client to actually follow through and implement the treatment plan or financial plan. Neither you nor I can force anyone to do anything. So if you have already had a financial plan prepared or are considering having a financial plan prepared, remember this; the best treatment plan in the world is useless if it is not actually implemented. The same goes for your financial plan. As Bill Bachrach says, having a financial plan and not implementing it, "is kind of like exercise; thinking about exercise does not actually improve your physical well-being. You have to actually exercise in order for it to work!" So even though a financial planner will show you what needs to be done and how to get it done, it will be up to you to actually follow through and "just do it!"

How to Pay Your Financial Planner

It goes without saying that anyone who provides a quality product or service deserves to be paid for it. At this point you may be wondering,

"How do financial planners actually get paid?" There are basically three types of planners:

- Commission-based financial planners
- Fee-only financial planners
- Asset-based financial planners

There are also those financial planners who combine two or even all three of these.

Below is a brief description of how each of these planners is paid along with some advantages and disadvantages of each. Let me preface this section by saying that one method of paying your advisor isn't necessarily better than another. You should, however, know in advance how your planner is being paid and agree in advance to the methodology for starting a professional relationship.

Commission-Based Financial Planners

Commission-based financial planners are compensated when you implement a portion of your financial plan that requires some sort of financial product: insurance or investment products, such as stocks, bonds or mutual funds.

The advantage of a commission-based planner is that you do not have to actually write a check to the planner. Instead, either an insurance company or an investment company with whom they place the financial products will pay them a commission. Generally speaking, the commission is paid up front and it is usually a one-time expense.

The disadvantage of this type of arrangement is that it may be difficult to know whether or not you are getting unbiased recommendations due to the fact that the advisor doesn't get paid unless you purchase some sort of financial product from them. In addition, once the planner has received the commission, there is little financial incentive left to continue to service your needs unless you have an ongoing need for commissioned based products. However, most good financial planners will continue to provide you service to maintain your current business with the potential of getting future business as well as possible referrals.

Fee-Only Financial Planners

Fee-only planners do not offer any financial products, but instead they may refer you to other advisors who do offer financial products: investment advisors, insurance agents, or you may use your own advisors for financial products.

Most fee-only financial planners charge an hourly rate, usually somewhere around $150–$250 per hour. An advantage of this type of arrangement is that you are only getting charged when the financial planner is actually working on your behalf; for instance, for a consultation, when they are preparing a financial plan, or at review time. The disadvantage of this type of arrangement is that you may get charged every time you talk to them, similar to an attorney.

My caution to you if you use a fee-only planner is this: When you know you will be charged when you ask a question, you may be less likely to make the phone call when you have a question. If you enter into an arrangement with a fee-only planner *you must be willing not only to pay by the hour, but also to make the phone call when you don't know the answer to your question.*

It may seem trite, but the only stupid question is the one you don't ask your financial planner. If you are going to enter into an arrangement with a fee-only financial planner, any and all major financial decisions should be addressed with your planner prior to making the decisions. This includes changing insurance coverage, changing estate plans, and making investment changes. Keeping your planner aware of what you are doing is vital to making a plan work. So you need to be prepared to make the phone call and pay the bill when your planner sends it to you!

Another type of fee-only planner is the flat fee financial planner. They may charge a flat (retainer) fee to design a financial plan and then charge an ongoing annual flat fee, to manage, update, and review your plan. The fees charged vary greatly and are usually based upon the complexity of the client's situation. An advantage of this type of arrangement is that you will know exactly what your annual costs are going to be. A disadvantage is that you might not get your money's worth year in and year out, depending on how much time your planner is actually working on your behalf. This type of arrangement is similar to a gym membership. Those who utilize the gym on a regular basis get more for their money than those who pay the gym membership fee, but don't go to the gym and exercise.

Asset-Based Financial Planners

Asset-based financial planners charge a fee based upon the amount of assets a client has. Some advisors will charge a fee based upon net worth and others will charge their fee based upon the assets (investments) being managed for the client by the planner. For instance, a fee-based planner might charge 1% on assets. If you have an investment portfolio of $500,000 on which your planner is charging one percent on assets under management, then you would be paying approximately $5,000 per year in planning fees. Most advisors prorate the fee out over four quarters (or six months) and will base the fee on the value of the assets at the end of the billing period. For instance, if the assets were valued at $500,000 on March 31 and the billing cycle is January 1–March 31, then the fee would be $1,250 in that quarter ($500,000 x 1% divided by 4). The fee is calculated quarterly, therefore it is based upon the value of the invested assets at the end of the quarter. With this type of arrangement, the fee will vary depending upon whether the value of the portfolio is increasing or decreasing.

The manner in which management fees are charged will vary from planner to planner. For instance, some may charge fees in arrears, while others charge fees in advance. In most cases, this won't make that big of a difference to your investment performance, so I wouldn't make this the deciding factor on which asset-based planner to use.

The disadvantage of this type of arrangement is that fees continue indefinitely or until the end of the relationship. The advantage of this arrangement is that the advisor has a vested interest in doing a good job for you, their client.

In summary, if you choose to use the services of a financial planner, you need to understand how you are going to pay for their services and then be willing to do so. Many financial planning firms use some combination of the above arrangements. Regardless of what type of financial planner you choose to work with, it is very important to know exactly how your financial planner gets paid so that there are no surprises!

My last point on this matter is this: don't be afraid to pay for good service and good advice. This is why you pay your CPA, your attorney, your realtor and your physician. So don't be afraid to pay your financial planner for his or her services and good advice. After all, isn't that what your patients are paying you for?

Why People Don't Plan

With all that we have discussed this far, why don't more people have a written financial plan that will help them to pursue what they really value in life? **Why don't people plan?**

• *Procrastination* is probably the biggest reason given for lack of planning. Many people will say, "I'll get around to it when..." When I get the building paid for or when the kids are out of school, when I get the bills paid, when I'm making more money and on and on they go. The longer you wait, the longer it will take you to reach your goals. I have seen more people make financial mistakes that could have easily been avoided if they would have simply taken the time to "do it" now. Ask yourself this question, "How much money or more importantly how much time am I losing by not doing it now?"

• *Ignorance.* Some people just don't know what to do. It's not that they are stupid. They simply don't know what to do. Well, I will tell you exactly what to do. Talk to several of your colleagues and/or other advisors such as your attorney or CPA. Obtain referrals from them in order to find a qualified financial planner, preferably a Certified Financial Planning® professional (CFP®). I recommend that you meet with two or three advisors to be sure you find someone that you (and your spouse, if you are married) feel has your best interest in mind and that you feel you would enjoy working with.

• *Fear of change.* That is they fear that if they go through the process of developing a comprehensive financial plan, they will discover that in order to achieve their goals for the future, they will have to change some things in their life today. That is, they may have to give something up to day in order to have something tomorrow. My response to the excuse is pretty simple. Get over it. I once heard someone say, "If you keep doin' what you've always done, you're gonna keep gettin' what you've always got."

Change is necessary in just about every facet of life. Personal health is a great example. If someone has had a problem with their weight and they continue to consume more calories than they burn, then they are going to continue to be overweight. The only way they are going to lose weight and keep it off is by burning more calories than they eat. This is not complicated. Losing weight for the vast majority is accomplished by exercise and an improved diet. Why do so many people struggle in this area then? Simply put, they don't want to change their lifestyle.

Personal finance is no different. In order to make smart choices with your money, change is most often going to be necessary. Remember, "If you keep doin' what you've always done, you're gonna keep gettin' what you always got."

• *Lack of accountability.* They don't want to be accountable to somebody else, not even a spouse or an advisor. They just don't want to be accountable to anybody else. I highly recommend you share your financial goals with someone. Preferably someone who will be a positive influence in helping you achieve them. I do this in many different areas of my own life. I share my financial goals with my advisors as well as some of my clients. I also have goals to continue to improve my personal relationships with my wife and children and I have mentors who I share these personal goals with. I apply these same principals to my spiritual and physical goals as well. Sharing your goals with someone else and becoming accountable outside yourself can be of tremendous value in helping you reach whatever type of goals you have. The truth is, most successful people, whether they are athletes, business people or ministers, have someone other than themselves they are accountable to.

• *Embarrassment.* I actually had a dentist tell me, "You know what Larry? I've known you for several years now and I know several people who are very happy with how you have been able to help them. The truth is, I'm embarrassed where I am financially." I was so amazed when this dentist said this to me. I wasn't amazed that he was embarrassed, but that he actually had the guts to admit it. The truth is, I think this is true for a lot of people, not just dentists. But remember, "If you keep doin' what you've always done, you're gonna keep gettin' what you've always got."

• *Trust.* They can't find anybody that they trust. Lack of trust is big and it keeps a lot of people from succeeding financially. However, it is my opinion that there are very few people who are capable of designing a successful financial plan without the help of a financial professional. Now, there is a big difference between a financial professional and sales-person in the financial services industry. So here are a few things to look for in selecting a *financial professional.*

First of all, a financial professional has a structured process for creating a financial plan for their clients and will be able to tell you what it is. It's not just about selling you an investment or insurance product. A financial professional will want to know about those things that are most important to you and not just talk about their services or the products they sell.

A financial professional will work very similarly to a CPA, attorney or your physician. They will want to review all of your financial data before making a recommendation. What would you think of a family doctor who handed you a prescription without finding out a lot of information about you? You'd probably think he was a quack. Your doctor will need to know about your medical history, allergies, family history, etc. Well, you should expect your financial professional to know what's important to you and to know your entire financial situation before making a recommendation. You should avoid an individual who is more interested in selling you a product than learning about what's most important to you.

You should be prepared to travel in order to meet a financial professional. Most sales people will travel anywhere to meet with anyone at anytime. A financial professional will want to meet in a professional environment and will generally require that anyone who shares in the financial decisions be involved in the process. Furthermore, the financial profes-sional will inspire you to achieve your goals and not prey on your fears and insecurities in order to get you to buy a product.

• *It costs too much.* If you are working with a qualified financial profes-sional this should not be the case. I say this because a qualified profes-sional should be able to provide you with more value than what their fee is. The same is true in dentistry, isn't it? The value received should always exceed the cost. Consider this. I generally base my fee on the complexity of a client's situation and I think this is true for many planners. So my recommendation would be to start planning before your situation becomes more complex. This will help to keep your costs down. In addition, it will help you avoid costly mistakes that may keep you from reaching your goals when you want.

I'm sure there are other reasons people don't plan, but I believe these cover the majority of the reasons I've heard over the years. I once heard an amusing story relating to excuses.

Bill heard a knock at his front door. He answered the door and there stood his next-door neighbor Bob. Bob, said, "Hi Bill. Can I borrow your chain saw?" Bill said, "No, Bob. I'm making chicken soup." Bob asked, "What's your making chicken soup have to do with me borrowing your chain saw, Bill?" To which Bill responded, "Nothing at all, Bob, but if I don't want you to borrow my chain saw, one excuse is as good as another." My point: Don't let excuses keep you from pursuing what you value most in life. Instead ask yourself this question, "How much is this excuse costing me in time and money?" Every excuse carries a price tag. What's yours?

The Story of a Young Dentist

This is the financial story of a young dentist and his wife who made some very smart decisions in the early years of his practice. It is a true story. The information I am sharing with you comes directly from their financial planning documents and I have worked with them for nearly ten years.

I met Thomas and Maggie in 1996. Thomas was in his second year of practice. He was and still is a sole practitioner. In 1996, Thomas' personal annual income was $52,000 (gross revenue less business expenses). At the time, Maggie was working and she was making $30,000 per year, so their combined household income was $82,000 per year.

Their 1996 net worth statement is on the next page.

In 1996, the market value of their home was $108,000 and they had a $95,000 mortgage. They had two cars worth $21,000 and they owed $10,000 on one of those vehicles. They had $10,000 in cash (checking) in his practice checking account and $7,000 in cash in their personal savings account. They had a (non-qualified) mutual fund account worth $861. Thomas also had a SEP IRA account invested in mutual funds worth $5,818. Their net worth in 1996 was $53,497.

When I met Thomas and Maggie in 1996, their primary goal was to be able to bring Maggie home full-time within two years and for Thomas to be able to retire at the age of 60 with a monthly income (adjusted for inflation) after taxes of $8,000 ($96,000 per year). They had no children, but they planned on having kids in the near future. They also wanted to buy a house that would cost them approximately $350,000 in five years. Those were the only two financial goals they had at that time.

1996 Personal Balance Sheet

USE ASSETS		$VALUE	PERSONAL LIABILITIES		
Residence	$	108,000	Residence	$	95,000
Auto #1		19,000	Auto #1		10,000
Auto #2		2,000			
			TOTAL PERSONAL		
TOTAL USE ASSETS	$	129,000	LIABILITIES	$	105,000
CASH RESERVES					
Personal Savings	$	7,000			
Money Market		-			
CD's					
Business Cash		10,000			
TOTAL CASH RESERVES	$	17,000			
GROWTH ASSETS					
IRA's, 401(k), Other Retirement	$	5,818			
Mutual Funds		861	BUSINESS LIABILITIES		
Dental Building		0	Dental Building	$	0
TOTAL GROWTH ASSETS	$	6,679			
OTHER ASSETS					
Cash Value Life Insurance	$	0			
Collectibles	$	0			
Others	$	0			
Total Other Assets	$	0	TOTAL LIABILITIES	$	105,000
TOTAL ALL ASSETS	$	158,497	NET WORTH	$	53,497

Let's see where they are now, nine years later. First of all, Thomas and Maggie now have two children ages 8 and 6. Thomas' personal annual income is $175,000 on gross practice revenue of $660,000. Thomas now works a 3½-day workweek. Maggie is at home full-time with their children and has been for several years. They are comfortably affording their new home (purchased in 2003) valued at $800,000. They have a 15-year mortgage with 13 years remaining. Thomas and Maggie did purchase their $350,000 house by the way, but have recently upgraded. The mortgage on their new home is $420,000, giving them $380,000 in equity in their home.

Thomas and Maggie own two cars worth approximately $35,000. Both vehicles are paid for. They have $55,000 in liquid savings. That includes his practice and their personal savings combined. They have stock/mutual fund investments valued at $78,300 plus $243,000 in retirement plan assets. Thomas is currently purchasing the building for his dental practice. The building is valued at approximately $650,000 and they owe $280,000 on the building, giving them a positive equity of $370,000 in the building.

Thomas and Maggie have saved $54,600 ($27,300 each) in their two children's college funds. In addition, they have accumulated $25,800 in Roth IRAs for the children. Thomas is now 38 years old and Maggie is 36 and their net worth is $1,488,300. It is important to note that their net worth does not include the value of the dental practice or personal items other than their vehicles. Below is the current Net Worth Statement.

Current Personal Balance Sheet

USE ASSETS		$VALUE	PERSONAL LIABILITIES		
Residence	$	800,000	Residence	$	380,000
Auto #1		20,000			
Auto #2		15,000			
Other Use Assets		12,000	TOTAL PERSONAL		
TOTAL USE ASSETS	$	847,000	LIABILITIES	$	380,000
CASH RESERVES					
Savings	$	12,000			
Money Market		15,000			
Checking		10,000			
Business Savings		40,000			
TOTAL CASH RESERVES	$	77,000			
GROWTH ASSETS					
IRA's, 401(k), Other Retirement	$	243,000			
Stocks, Bonds, Mutual Funds		78,300	BUSINESS LIABILITIES		
Dental Building		660,000	Dental Building	$	280,000
TOTAL GROWTH ASSETS	$	981,300			

Current Personal Balance Sheet (continued)

OTHER ASSETS
Cash Value Life Insurance
Collectibles
Others

Total Other Assets	$	0	TOTAL LIABILITIES	$	660,000
TOTAL ALL ASSETS	**$ 2,148,300**		**NET WORTH**	**$**	**1,488,300**

Thomas and Maggie are currently on track to be 100% debt free, including the office building and their home by the time Thomas is 48 years old, just 11 years from now.

Thomas and Maggie's retirement goals have changed. Their current goal is for Thomas to retire on June 1, 2023 (he will be 55 years old) with an inflation-adjusted after-tax monthly income of $10,000 per month. Remember, they will be DEBT FREE seven years prior to that date. And their children will most likely be out of college by then. They have a very high probability of achieving this goal.

In 1996, Thomas was twenty-eight years old and in his second year of practice. He and Maggie had simple financial goals and their finances were not that complicated. But even so, we still went through the process of designing a comprehensive financial plan. Why? For the same reason you would design a comprehensive treatment plan for any patient of yours, in order to achieve the greatest likelihood of achieving their goals. They started early and proceeded with their plan and made changes along the way as they were needed or desired.

In addition to planning for their own retirement, they have even begun to fund their children's retirement plans. I asked Thomas what was important about helping his children fund their retirement plans. He said that he wanted to give his kids the option to pursue the career that they wanted. "Basically I want to be able to provide my children the option to pursue their passion and not have to worry so much about funding their retirement." If my daughter wants to be a teacher, or marry a teacher and be a stay-at-home mom, I want her to be able to pursue what she values most. By saving for her retirement now, I feel as though I am giving her a better chance to be able to that. And as uncertain as Social Security is for us, imagine what it's going to be like for them." Talk about living a life of value! What a tremendous impact Thomas and Maggie could possibly have, not on just their children, but on future generations as well.

The success that Thomas and Maggie are experiencing is not just because of my great planning. (Though I'd like to believe my encouragement and direction has helped them to make smart financial decisions along the way.) The major reason they are doing so well is due to the fact that they started early and they implemented their financial plan early on. My point in stressing the word implemented is this. Having a written financial plan and not actually implementing it, is kind of like exercise; thinking about starting an exercise program, and even having an exercise program designed by a fitness trainer is worthless if you don't actually exercise! The same goes for your financial plan. Spending the time and money to have a financial plan designed especially for you to help you achieve what is most important to you in life is meaningless if you don't actually follow-through and implement your plan.

Another important point I want to make sure to get across is the fact that Thomas and Maggie have always lived within their income. They never increased their lifestyle until they could really afford to. They made smart, calculated, thought-out decisions with the help of their professional advisors. Yes, they sometimes sacrificed, but they are being rewarded for doing so and I am confident that they will continue to be rewarded for these smart decisions well into their future!

In addition, it is important for you to know that Thomas and Maggie have carried all the appropriate levels of insurance coverages (life, health, disability, business overhead insurance, malpractice, personal and business property and casualty insurance, umbrella insurance). They also have all of the appropriate estate-planning documents that are appropriate for their personal situation.

Thomas and Maggie are what I refer to as fully engaged clients and that is another reason they are well on their way to reaching their goals. They have chosen to use a financial planner (me in this case) as well as other professional advisors so that they are free to pursue their interests as well as to allow them to enjoy the time they have together as a family.

You know, its kind of funny. I was talking with a physician the other day and he was expressing his frustrations about his patients who don't follow his recommendations. Why does he get so frustrated? Because he strongly believes that his patient's health will be greatly improved if they will just follow his treatment plan. I have heard many similar frustrations as dental professionals and physical therapists echo these comments. Why people think managing the financial part of their life is any different is a mystery to me. Maybe it's because they think that money is a renewable resource and they will always be able to earn more. For some people this may be true, but I don't think so for the vast majority of people. And even if money were a renewable resource, time surely is not.

As a dental professional you have the opportunity to earn a tremendous amount of money over your working lifetime. If you think that you will accumulate enough money to enjoy a comfortable retirement, pay for your kid's college education (if that's a goal of yours), have your estate distributed according to your desires or that any other financial goal is going to be achieved without proper planning, you are in for a major shock.

Yes, financial planning takes time and cost money. It also takes a desire to do things right and it takes a commitment to implement your financial plan. It doesn't just happen. You have got to make it happen. As a dental professional you know the value of a properly implemented treatment plan. I am confident that a professionally designed financial treatment plan will provide tremendous value to you as well.

Delegate Things to Improve Quality Of Life

I thoroughly enjoy living in the Arizona desert, but I also enjoy having a nice green lawn. Believe it or not, there was a time when I had actually convinced myself that I enjoyed mowing my grass. Now I do enjoy working outside, but did I really enjoy mowing grass in Phoenix, Ariz., in the summer when it was 110 degrees? I don't think so, but somehow, I had convinced myself that I did. For years I spent my Saturdays mowing my yard and trimming our trees and shrubs. Now I'm not saying that it is a waste of time to mow your own lawn and take care of your own landscaping. What I discovered for me, though, it wasn't so much the work I enjoyed, but more the finished product; a beautiful yard. After having this "epiphany," I immediately looked into hiring someone to take care of my landscaping. I discovered that I would much rather pay someone else to mow my yard and enjoy my Saturdays in the swimming pool with my wife and kids.

Something else I really enjoy about having someone else do my yard work is that, in my case, they actually do the work on Friday rather than the weekend. It's especially nice during the summer months. Why? I come home on Friday afternoon after enjoying a day on the lake with my family and the yard is mowed. I share this with you as an illustration of the value of delegation. We all have something that we value in life. As I shared earlier in this book, I mentioned how much I enjoy spending Friday's on the lake with my family in the summer. It's nice to come home from a day on the lake to a freshly mowed yard, knowing that on Saturday morning I don't have to get up and do it myself. Sure, I have to pay my landscaper, but to me it's well worth the price, because it allows me to enjoy something that I truly value in life.

Who performs these tasks in your office? Answering the phone, setting patient appointments, verifying insurance coverage? I would bet that if you are a dentist, it's not you. Why not? That's simple; these are office functions that are most appropriately delegated to someone else. Because delegating these functions frees up time for you to spend where it is used most effectively and most profitably; with your patients designing and implementing treatment plans.

Of course, not everything can be delegated. For instance, you can't delegate good health, or your spiritual life. You can't delegate being a role model for your children and you can't delegate nurturing family relationships. However, just as you delegate certain job functions in order to be more productive and profitable in your practice, I encourage you to look closely at financial planning tasks that you are currently trying to do yourself and delegate them to a qualified financial professional. In doing so, you will free up time to do things that matter most to you. Perhaps this will even allow you to pursue some other personal goal you've always wanted to, but just haven't had the time.

Don't Miss the View

As I close this last chapter I'd like to leave you with one last illustration of the value of having a written financial plan that is professionally designed to help you live out the values and achieve the goals that are most important to you.

In January 2001, I was invited by Jim and Naomi Rhode (founders of Smart Practice) to speak at their annual conference in Hawaii on the island of Kauai. My wife Rhonda and I had never been to Hawaii before and we were very excited to be going. The conference was fantastic with several exceptional speakers. I was especially honored and thrilled to be on the same speaking platform with Jim and Naomi, both of whom have served as past president of the National Speaker's Association.

While on the island, Rhonda and I enjoyed some of the most beautiful scenery in the world. One part of the trip that was especially memorable for me was a one-hour helicopter tour of the island of Kauai. As we boarded the helicopter, we were each handed a headset and told that it would reduce the noise from the helicopter as well as allow us to listen to our pilot who would also be our tour guide. Before our take off, our Australian pilot (this was easy to tell from his accent) greeted each passenger by name. When he got to me he said, "Good afternoon Mr. Mathis, I'm glad to have you with us today, however before we take off I'd like to make a suggestion. I see you've brought along your video camera. Now it's all right with me if you want to use it, however I think it's important to point out a couple of things to you.

You are about to embark on a bird's eye, scenic tour of one of the most beautiful islands in the world. If you intend to film this tour, let me tell you what you can expect. First of all, the film quality will most likely be very poor, due to the fact that we often experience some bumpiness along the way: and it will be especially poor if you intend to use the zoom feature on your camera. Furthermore, the sound of the helicopter rotor won't make for very good background noise. In addition, it's not uncommon for passengers to become airsick when using video equipment while we are in the air, so when we land you will likely have a mess to cleanup and the other passengers may not enjoy the tour as much should you get sick and throw-up. Most importantly, however, when the tour is over you're going to realize that you missed the whole thing by looking through that little viewfinder. My suggestion, Mr. Mathis, would be that if you want to take this tour home with you to enjoy again at another time, stop by our gift shop after we land and purchase a professionally filmed video of the tour for about 20 bucks. The videography is superb and includes a tremendous soundtrack along with it."

In summary what he said to me was this, if you want to "do it yourself" go ahead, but most likely you will end up with poor results, a mess to clean up and you'll miss the view you came to see in the first place. I took his recommendation and put my video camera away and I must say it was truly a spectacular tour; one that I will never forget.

My point in telling this story is this. You can choose to do your own financial planning, but I caution you just as my helicopter pilot cautioned me. You may very well end up with poor results, a mess to clean up and along the way you'll miss a lot of life's view.

In closing, I would like to encourage you that wherever you are right now, whether you're just getting started or you have been practicing for many years, take a close look at what you really want out of life. Determine what you value most in life, hire a financial planning profes-sional, set your goals to writing and develop a comprehensive financial plan. Then implement your plan! Lastly, don't do everything yourself. Delegate whatever you can to your professional advisors and enjoy life's view along the way.

Get Started Now - Free Planning Tools

These planning tools will get you headed in the right direction. Whether you're just getting started in the dental profession, or if you are preparing for retirement from this great profession, knowing where you stand financially is essential.

As a dental professional, you know the importance of the initial evaluation of a new patient. It tells you the status of the patient's oral health, right? And, without an initial evaluation there is no way to develop a treatment plan. Just as there are essential tools for performing an initial exam on a patient (explorer, hand mirror, periodontal probe, radiographs), there are also essential tools that are needed to determine your current financial health:

1. Financial document checklist – The documents contained in this checklist (as they pertain to you) are essential to preparing a comprehensive financial plan. Once you have these documents together you are well on your way to getting started.

2. List of assets and list of debts worksheets – These worksheets when completed will help you develop your personal balance sheet, which in essence will tell you your net worth. In addition these worksheets will assist you in developing your debt elimination plan.

3. Expense summary worksheet – This worksheet will help you develop your personal cash flow statement. Knowing where your money is going is key to financial success! And this important financial tool is foundational to good financial hygiene.

To get your free copy of these valuable tools go to www.BridgingtheFinancialGap.com. Take the time to do it now and if you have any questions please don't hesitate to contact me.

Now What?

Okay, so you've finished reading, *Bridging the Financial Gap for Dentists* and you've taken the time to go to get your free planning tools at www.BridgingTheFinancialGap.com. So what do you do now?

First of all, if you haven't already done so, take time to evaluate what is really important to you. And if you're married, I strongly suggest that you go through the process illustrated in the values chapter together. Remember, clearly identifying your values (those things you value most in life) will help inspire you to achieve the goals you set for yourself and motivate you to follow through with the implementation of your comprehensive financial plan.

Once you've determined what you value most, begin setting your financial goals as outlined in Chapter 3. Be sure not to leave out any steps in the goal setting process.

The next thing you should do is to develop your personal balance sheet and your Personal Cash Flow Statement. Your free planning tools (see list below) when completed will give you all of the information you will need to complete these financial statements.
1. Financial documents checklist
2. List of assets worksheet
3. List of debts worksheet
4. Expense summary worksheet

Once you have completed the above steps then you need to find a financial planning professional to help you develop your comprehensive financial plan. Remember this needs to be a person who does comprehensive financial planning, not someone who merely sells financial products. You need to find a qualified financial planning professional, preferably a Certified Financial Planner™ professional. To find a planner in your area I suggest that you either obtain referrals from your colleagues, CPA or other advisors, or you may also contact me directly and I will be happy to help you find a financial planning professional who can help you. I have listed my contact information below:

Larry L. Mathis, CFP®
7210 N. 16th Street
Phoenix, AZ 85020
(602) 393-0501 or (800) 817-9406
Larry@BridgingTheFinancialGap.com

In my introduction, I stated that my goals were to:

1. Help you avoid costly mistakes that may prevent you from achieving your personal and financial goals in the time frame you are hoping for.
2. Assist you in maximizing your wealth potential, by making smart choices with your money, regardless of where you stand financially at this moment.
3. Help you discover how to live your life based upon those things that you value most and inspire you to develop a financial strategy to help you enjoy them to the fullest.

Ultimately it is my hope that *Bridging the Financial Gap for Dentists* will simplify and improve the lives of dental professionals by inspiring them to implement financial strategies based upon those things that are most important to them in life.

I hope that you have discovered that this book has in some way achieved one or all of these goals for you. If you have any comments or suggestions on how this book can be improved or how I can be of individual help to you, I welcome the opportunity to talk with you personally.

Who the Heck is Larry Mathis?

In my years as an insurance agent, investment advisor and ultimately financial planner, I have often hosted what I refer to as Client Appreciation Events. One year, I held a sit-down dinner at the Arizona Country Club for 180 clients and guests. During this event, I had invited an investment guru from Boston to be our featured guest speaker. Well, for some reason he had to cancel at the last minute. So instead of the guru, the company for which he worked scrambled to find someone to send in his place as to not let me down.

Low and behold the only person in the company who had the evening available was none other than the president of the company. The story goes that he walked to his office in Boston the morning of the event and was advised that he would be flying to Phoenix, Ariz. to speak at an event for a client of their firm (me). He wasn't taken with the idea due to the fact that he had just flown back to Boston the night before from Phoenix. (He had been in Scottsdale, Ariz. on business.)

His staff told him it was important that he return to Phoenix in order to speak at a client appreciation dinner being sponsored by Larry Mathis. His response, "Who the heck is Larry Mathis?" This story as I relate to you, were his opening remarks that evening at my client appreciation dinner, along with the now famed question (among several of my clients) that you too may be asking, "Who the heck, is Larry Mathis?"

Well, let me tell you. I am Larry Mathis. I am a native of Phoenix, Ariz. I was born to Gerald D. Mathis and Jeannine S. Mathis. In 1965, my father died, leaving my 35-year mother with my five sisters, my older brother and me to raise on her own. Much of what I know about personal finance I learned from my mother (but that's another book.)

I graduated from Arizona State University with a Bachelor of Science Degree in Agricultural Business. Upon graduation from ASU in 1984, I went to work for the Ciba-Geigy Corporation (a large multi-national conglomerate based in Basil Switzerland). In 1985, I was married to my wife, Rhonda, and within days of our wedding, Ciba-Geigy moved us to San Diego, Calif.

It was in San Diego where I was introduced to the life insurance business by a gentleman named, Ben Lontock. Later I was to discover that Ben was one of the top 300 life insurance agents in the world! After living in San Diego for about four years, Rhonda and I decided to move back to Phoenix to be closer to our families. Shortly thereafter, I left Ciba-Geigy to become a full-time insurance agent. At that time I became a disability insurance specialist for the Paul Revere Life Insurance Company.

It was during my years with Paul Revere that I focused my marketing efforts within the dental profession. (By the way, thank you to Sam Post and Dave Lavin who taught me more about disability insurance than you can possibly imagine.) After selling disability insurance to dentists for about two years, I discovered something. There is only so much disability insurance that a dentist can buy, and my limited experience and education, also limited the services I could provide to my clients. It was about that time when I decided that I wanted to become a "real" financial planner. I decided that I needed more education and training in the field of personal finance. Well, to make a long-story short, for the next several years I worked for several insurance-based financial planning organizations. And though in and of themselves they were fine companies, they were companies that were very oriented to pushing insurance-based products (mainly life-insurance) to meet the needs of my clients.

Now understand, I am a big believer in life insurance. The fact is it was life insurance that kept our family living on the right side of the tracks when my father died. It was life insurance that fed our family and housed our family. And it was life insurance that paid for my college education. However, life insurance is not the answer to all financial planning needs.

During my years with various insurance companies, I also went through the processes of getting my series 6, 63, 7 and 65 licenses that allowed me to sell stocks, bonds, mutual funds and securities-based insurance products. It was also during these years that I met Dennis Rogers. Dennis was a CPA who had the same goal to provide comprehensive financial planning.

Dennis and I later formed Rogers, Mathis & Associates, an independent financial planning firm in Phoenix, Ariz. Eventually we brought on Frank Kirby as a third partner and Rogers, Mathis & Kirby was formed.

Today, I operate my personal financial planning practice as a sole practitioner specializing in helping dental professionals *Bridge the Financial Gap.* I am dedicated to providing comprehensive financial planning services to dental professionals. As a Certified Financial Planner™ I focus my efforts on helping dental professionals improve their lives as well as the lives of their families both personally and financially. It is my goal that the information shared in this book will do the same for you.

Printed in the USA
CPSIA information can be obtained
at www.ICGtesting.com
JSHW082213140824
68134JS00014B/605